# When Ministers SIN

## Sexual Abuse in the Churches

Neil and Thea Ormerod

MILLENNIUM BOOKS

First published by
Millennium Books
an imprint of E.J. Dwyer (Australia) Pty Ltd
Unit 13, Perry Park
33 Maddox Street
Alexandria NSW 2015
Australia
Phone: (02) 550-2355
Fax: (02) 519-3218

Distributed in the U.S. by Seven Hills Book Distributors
49 Central Avenue
CINCINNATI OH 45202

National Library of Australia
Cataloguing-in-Publication data

Ormerod, Neil.
    When ministers sin.

    Bibliography.
    ISBN 1 86429 011 0.
    1. Clergy — Sexual behavior. 2. Sex crimes. 3. Sex — Religious
    aspects. 4. Clergy — Professional ethics. 5. Sexual ethics.
    I. Ormerod, Thea, 1955–   . II. Title.

261.833153

Cover design by Simon Leong
Cover illustration by Thea Ormerod
Text design by Warren Penney
Typeset in Garamond 11/14pt by Sun Photoset Pty Ltd, Brisbane
Printed in Australia by Australian Print Group, Maryborough,
Victoria

10 9 8 7 6 5 4 3 2 1

99 98 97 96 95

# CONTENTS

We would like to dedicate this book to E.P.N., whose sensitivity and care have been a source of strength for us all.

# ACKNOWLEDGMENTS

As in any project such as this, there are numerous people who have provided invaluable assistance in bringing it to completion. We would like to thank our friends in Friends of Susanna, a Sydney-based survivors' advocacy group, who have provided help and encouragement. Thanks also to Helen Last and Anne Hall of Project Anna, from the Centre Against Sexual Assault in Melbourne, who have provided support, encouragement and the numerous articles and references which have filled out our own experiences. Thanks finally to our friends and especially our young children who have had to put up with their parents' working on such a time-consuming project for so long.


Use of material with the permission of the publishers or copyright holders is gratefully acknowledged as follows:

*Suffer the Children: A Theology of Liberation by a Victim of Child Abuse*, Janet Pais, published by and copyright 1991, Paulist Press (Mahwah).

Excerpt from "Little Gidding", in *Four Quartets*, copyright 1943 by T. S. Eliot and renewed 1971 by Esme Valerie Eliot; reprinted by permission of Harcourt Brace & Co. and Faber and Faber Ltd (London).

# FOREWORD

In this book are powerful and authentic stories of betrayal. The betrayal is devastating because it comes from the Body of Christ, the church, which holds out such a promise of truth, love and justice in the name of its God. If it is not to be trusted, then who can we trust?

Why do these stories need to be told? Are they not the private property of the church as it deals with human sinfulness among its employees? The church has never pretended that its clergy are other than human. Does not this airing of our failures do damage to the church?

I believe that it is now critical to hear, with clarity, the living witness of the people of this book. In the agony of their experience, they are inviting the church to face the truth and to accept corporate responsibility for its own life. We are a Body, not a group of individuals expressing our devotion to God. We dare to claim that we are the Body of Christ. At the very center of our faith is the life and death of Jesus Christ who leads us firmly into the center of our deaths and shows us that there is no other path to fullness of life. Over and over again, we are taught by Christ that only the truth will set us free and that we need not be afraid if we will face our realities, safe in the grace of God.

This does not mean, of course, that the primary call is to offer grace and forgiveness to those who violate and abuse others. If the righteous anger of God is not expressed in our clear solidarity with the abused, then, I believe, we do not create the safe journey towards grace for the abuser. The most terrifying feature of evil is that it usually comes disguised as good. We do not offer authentic grace to those who are bound into abusive lives unless we carry them firmly and rigorously into reality and invite them into the costly and painful journey towards rebirth in the Spirit. True love is never based on protecting people from their own truths because if we do that we hold them in their own deaths instead of the rigor of growth towards maturity, freedom and peace.

This is, as I said, a corporate journey. As we look at the sub-culture of violence and abuse that lies within our whole society and face that it also runs through the life of the church, we cannot avoid asking the essential questions about the source of this evil. Why is this violation there? Why do we try to hide it when we are so open about other damage to ourselves, such as burglary, physical assault in our streets and theft of our cars? Are we afraid to name the violation of our deepest beings, the betrayal of our most sacred trusts? Does it raise questions about our teachings and underlying assumptions about the right relationship between women and men?

This book raises, in almost every story, the issue of power in human relationships. In many ways it is not a book about sexual misdemeanor. One of the important reasons for its publication is the repeated failure of the church to face this issue. It is so easy to dismiss claims of abuse between adults if we discount the issue of imbalance of power. These stories face all clergy, and all those involved in client or professional relationships (or both), with the need to come to terms with their grave responsibility and to develop a healthy and honest relationship with their own sexuality.

This book is also needed as a validation of the life experience of those who have been abused—to name for them the truth of their own reality and point to where real responsibility lies. It is needed as an encouragement for them to be open to their own truth, to seek the support they deserve, to come for healing and to claim life in all its fullness again.

Most of all, this book is an invitation to the church to believe what we say we believe—that God is always there for us, with us, around us and within us if we dare to look truth in the face and move towards justice. We will never be whole until we do.

Dorothy McRae-McMahon
*National Director for Mission*
*Uniting Church in Australia.*

# INTRODUCTION

This has been a very difficult book for us to write. It arises out of more than a year's experience with survivors of sexual abuse by church ministers, particularly through the survivors' group called Friends of Susanna. Any naïvety that we may have had with regard to the churches has been stripped away by this experience. It is not as if we ever thought the churches had no problems, far from it. What has been so difficult is to experience the depth of those problems. The churches have found themselves unable to respond in even a human, let alone Christian, manner to those who come forward with disclosures of sexual abuse by church ministers.[1] While the churches, at least some, are beginning to work towards an adequate response, their present and past failures are a sign of how far many of them are from understanding the message of Jesus. An over-spiritualized understanding of faith has promoted a view of religious life which does not touch on the basic realities of human existence.

The Christian message talks about love, forgiveness, healing, justice and mercy. Church leaders can be very articulate in speaking about the Christian message, putting all the words in the right order, speaking with all the eloquence of angels. Yet, too often, the love and forgiveness that they speak of exists only in a world of romantic illusion. It is not the love, forgiveness, healing, justice and mercy of real human relationship. In the real world such things are costly, hard-won and painful. They do not

---

[1] Throughout this book we have deliberately spoken of "disclosures" rather than "allegations." Church authorities often worry about "false allegations." We believe that this is an overrated fear. Survivors often have far more to lose by bringing forward disclosures than they have to gain.

come about by speaking about them, but by doing them. In the area of sexual abuse by its ministers, church leaders too often prove themselves capable only of talk, not of action, as if talk alone can create the reality. They get caught up in patterns of behavior which serve to "protect" perpetrators and further harm survivors. They put the legal and financial concerns of the institution, and protecting the church from scandal, before the demands of justice for those who have suffered at the hands of church ministers.

The problem of sexual abuse by church ministers is not new. It has probably been around from the very beginning. Certainly the misogyny of the early church Fathers would have provided ample background for patterns of abuse to emerge. Yet it is a problem which is only beginning to gain attention. Why is this so?

Here credit must be given to the brave men and women who have dared to break the silence on the issue of incest and sexual abuse in the family. As is well known, when Freud began his investigations in depth psychology, he was shocked by the number of patients who reported sexual abuse in childhood. When he discussed his findings with colleagues they convinced him that this could not be true. He eventually decided that such reports must be childhood fantasies. One colleague in particular, Wilhelm Fliess, was instrumental in helping Freud change his mind. It was later revealed that Fliess had sexually abused his own son![2] It has taken courage and determination by incest survivors to break through the defenses of denial and minimization that have operated for millennia to protect incestuous fathers. They have had to fight the legal system, the psychiatric profession and a culture that simply does not want to know.

In many ways the situation of sexual abuse in the churches is analogous to that of incest. Indeed the churches often use the rhetorical symbolism of family. Sexual abuse is a secret that no-one wants to know about. It is too awful, too dark, too ugly to acknowledge. Better to pretend it doesn't exist. And if it does—it's not common; it's probably the victim's fault; the poor minister

---

[2] See Alice Miller, *Banished Knowledge: Facing Childhood Injuries*, (New York; Anchor Books, 1990), pp.55–56.

was over-worked and looking for affection; he was trapped into celibacy; his wife didn't understand him. The list of excuses goes on and on. Like incest survivors before them, survivors of sexual abuse by ministers have to have courage and determination to break through the silence, the denial and trivialization that surround the issue. We can only hope that the churches will be prepared to listen.

Throughout this book we speak of the minister as "he" and the victim as "she." This is not to imply that women should not be ministers or that men cannot be victims of abuse, or even that women cannot abuse. However we have opted to speak this way as we believe it to be the more statistically normal case.

## AN ISSUE FOR THE CHURCHES TODAY

Sexual abuse is one of the major issues of the 1990s. Across the English-speaking world one church community after another is being torn apart by disclosures of sexual abuse or misconduct by men who have been well-loved and well-respected leaders of their communities. As more and more survivors of abuse come forward, the churches have repeatedly shown themselves unable to respond adequately to their pain and their thirst for justice. Legal and financial constraints have hemmed in church leaders, who are afraid of the institutional consequences of dealing openly and honestly with the problem.

The churches have begun to develop public policies and procedures for dealing with disclosures of abuse. Some have been in consultation with survivors' groups which have arisen in response to church failures in the past. It is to be hoped that all church communities can begin to take the issue more seriously, to overcome the initial stages of denial and begin to address the questions of abuse at all levels within their communities. However, even the best policies and procedures will mean nothing unless the underlying attitudes of those who administer them are changed.

This book is a contribution to the debate on sexual abuse in the churches. It has been written primarily to give voice to the experience of survivors of abuse by church ministers. In any debate theirs is the voice which must first be heard and listened to with respect. Because it is written from the perspective of survivors it will not cover every aspect of the issue, nor will the coverage it does give satisfy those who are looking for a "balanced" point of view. It unashamedly takes the role of advocate, standing with victims. We shall let others speak for the institutional concerns of the churches.

As part of the debate, we hope that this book will reach various groups. Firstly, we hope that it will be read by survivors of abuse. We hope that they will find their experiences validated and affirmed. We hope that they will learn what to expect from the churches if they seek justice and so be forewarned. Secondly, we hope that this book will be read by those responsible for the development of church policies and procedures. Undoubtedly they will find it an uncomfortable book, but unless they are able to face the discomfort they will never be able to respond adequately. Thirdly, we hope that this book will be read by those who counsel survivors of sexual abuse by church ministers. Though there are parallels with other forms of abuse, there are dimensions which distinctively belong to such abuse and counselors need to be aware of them.

Finally, but not of least importance, we hope that this book will be read by those involved in the training of ministers and by those they train. Until the issue of sexual abuse is dealt with explicitly and separately from other issues it will not be dealt with properly and those involved in training will be remiss in their responsibilities to their church communities. In the end it will be the training of future ministers in the issue of sexual abuse that will be instrumental in shifting the attitudes which lie at the heart of abuse. Ministers need to be aware that they are persons of power, indeed divine power, and the misuse of this power is central to the problem of sexual abuse. As the feminists say of rape, "it's not about sex, it's about power." When ministers abuse their pastoral position for their own sexual advantage they pervert what should be a position of healing into an instrument of destruction. These are the messages those who are training for ministry need to hear and they need to hear them loud and clear.

## WHAT IS SEXUAL ABUSE?[3]

For many the term has horrific significance and this is well justified. However it need not be thought of in terms of assault or
violence. To abuse someone or something is to use that person or
thing in a manner which is not appropriate. As with many things
there are gradations of activities which constitute sexual abuse,
from harassment to assault. However whatever these gradations
may be, only survivors can know the extent of the damage done
to them by these activities.

> *An abusive act or relationship is one which causes
> unnecessary or unwarranted hurt to another person*

Such action may be of a physical, sexual or psychological nature.
There may be circumstances where hurt is necessary or warranted,
for example, the surgeon's removal of a gangrenous limb, the therapist's recall of a painful memory, an act of self-defense. However
an abusive act is unwarranted. Whatever the rationalizations of the
abuser, his actions are not justified by the perceived good either to
himself or to the other.

> *An abusive act may be either intentional or unintentional*

An intentional act of abuse is basically sadistic. It deliberately
seeks to do harm for the pleasure of harming another. This, however, is relatively rare. The more common problem is not one of
intention, but inattention. The person is simply unaware that they
are doing harm. They are not attentive to the suffering of the other
person. Indeed they may even think of themselves as doing good
to the other. For example, a patronizing act may be quite abusive,
even with the "best intentions" in the world. As common wisdom
states, the path to hell is paved with good intentions.

---

[3] This material is based on insights from Marie Fortune, *Is Nothing Sacred?: The
Story of a Pastor, the Women he Sexually Abused, and the Congregation he Nearly
Destroyed* (Harper San Francisco, 1989); Peter Rutter, *Sex in the Forbidden Zone:
When Men in Power—Therapists, Doctors, Clergy, Teachers and others—Betray
Women's Trust*, (London; Mandala, 1989); and Karen Lebacqz and Ronald
G. Barton, *Sex in the Parish* (Louisville; Westminister/John Knox Press, 1991).
These are the three key books in the area of pastoral sexual abuse and we
acknowledge our debt to them here and throughout this book.

*\* The damage done in an abusive act or relationship will depend on the power differential between the two persons*

The more powerful the abusive person is, the more damage he is likely to do. The more powerful he is, the greater his responsibility to act for the good of the other person. Power also means that the abused person is likely to put greater antecedent trust in the abuser. The abused person will see the abuser as someone who may be able to help her in some problem. It is the abuse of this trust which can do great damage. Also the greater the power differential, the more difficult it will be for the abused person to free herself from the abuse. She will feel trapped in the relationship, unable to break free.

*\* Power can be of two types, personal or structural*

Personal power can be a matter of physical strength, psychological invulnerability, charisma or simply age difference. Structural power is a matter of a formal relationship which exists between the two persons, such as a parent–child, therapist–client, minister–congregant and so on. Some persons will, of course, be powerful in more than one sense.

*\* Sexual abuse is any act which eroticizes a relationship between two persons of unequal power, leading to harm to the less powerful person*

Sexual abuse does not necessarily imply genital activity. It can be any act which erodes the sexual boundary between the two persons, for example, sexual innuendo, kissing, unwanted or unnecessary touching of buttocks or breasts, overly long hugs and so on. It can involve apparently consensual sexual intercourse but, as Fortune notes,[4] the validity of consent is negated by the power differential. At its worst it involves sexual assault.

## THIS BOOK

The purpose of this book is to study the nature and consequences of such acts when they occur within a ministerial setting, where the abuser is a church minister and the abused is someone in his

---

[4] Fortune, p.37ff.

pastoral care. This person may be either a child or an adult. In either case there is a power differential as we have defined it above. Whether he is aware of it or not, the minister has structural power, a power commensurate with his position as a minister. He is used to "running the show", to getting, or at least expecting, to get what he wants, to being the leader of the community. To this might be added that he is an adult male and hence possesses a physical strength and social status greater than children and women. He may possess psychological strength or other forms of psychological invulnerability as well. To this we must add that the minister is seen as God's representative and one doesn't get much more powerful than that! Ministers share in a numinous power and it is naïve to think that they are not aware of this and in fact enjoy it. All this can add up to a potent force and a considerable power differential between the minister and those in his pastoral care.

We should also note the extraordinary amount of trust which the ministers carry. They are seen as men of God by the Christian community and are generally respected members of the broader community. They are thought to be of higher moral standing than the normal run of humankind and, at least within the Catholic tradition, to be celibate. People trust them to be morally upright. As is the case in all forms of sexual abuse, the greater the trust the greater the damage done to the victims.

While the situation of child sexual abuse has been the one which has received most attention, both in the media and in terms of church response, much of the analysis presented here deals more directly with the situation of adult sexual abuse, for this is the aspect which the churches have yet to adequately recognize. This is not to minimize the situation of child sexual abuse or its horrific consequences. Hopefully survivors of either form of sexual abuse will recognize common patterns of abuse, its consequences and the way in which the churches handle disclosures. Indeed one of the points of this book is that both forms of abuse can be very damaging since the nature of the abuse is the same.

The book itself is divided into two sections. Part One deals with various dimensions of the issue of sexual abuse by church ministers. Part Two has been supplied to us by a number of survivors and support persons. These are their stories, in their own words. They are words of pain and suffering, of trust abused, of confrontation and, occasionally, of hope. Those who have been there will recognize their words as true. The first part of the book also contains poems written by a survivor and other material illustrative of points made in the text.

We are extremely grateful to those survivors who have provided us with this material and we hope this book gives them due honor. At all stages we have tried to be careful not to use material without the permission of those involved.

Inevitably a book of this nature, which contains material from actual cases, raises concerns especially for publishers seeking to avoid legal problems. We have taken pains to ensure that identifying facts have been changed in order to conceal the true identity of survivors and their abusers. Anyone who seeks to make such identifications is patently missing the point of the book, which is not to damage reputations, but to enter into the experience of survivors. We apologize to anyone who feels they may be identifiable by material in this book, despite or even because of our efforts to change details. Indeed we believe that the events in this book are so common that no individual should feel singled out![5]

---

[5] For example, when Australia's national broadcaster (the ABC) screened a dramatized account of sexual abuse, they were contacted by a number of different persons each claiming that their case had been used without permission.

# PART ONE

PART ONE

# CHAPTER ONE

# PASTORAL SEXUAL

## ABUSE

S ex, religion and politics are three areas of human living which tend to stir up strong passions. When two of these converge on a single point, the result is a heady mixture which draws considerable media interest. Perhaps the most explosive mixture is that of sex and religion, which invariably attracts extensive media coverage, sometimes on a global scale. Such attention delights at the hypocrisy displayed by those who publicly uphold high standards of sexual morality yet whose private lives have been hotbeds of sexual impropriety. Within the Catholic Church these issues are complicated by a vow of celibacy or chastity[1] which is seen as further compounding the hypocrisy involved.

Yet the issues at stake are not just those of sexual morality and celibacy. Those involved in ministry are placed in positions of special responsibility towards those under their care, so it is far more an issue of the ethics of a professional carer in relation to those under his or her care. Under such circumstances the sexual impropriety of a priest or minister can easily become a matter of abusing the power of his privileged office for sexual ends. This constitutes a sexual abuse of those entrusted to his pastoral care. Following

---

[1] One may distinguish between a promise of celibacy which is demanded as part of the church's discipline for priesthood and a religious vow of chastity which is part of the consecrated life-style of a religious community. Thus a religious priest who engages in sexual relations violates not only a promise expressive of the church's discipline. He also violates the religious spirit of his community. However in this book we shall refer loosely to a "vow of celibacy" to cover both cases.

an article by Reverend Pamela Cooper-White, we shall refer to this as pastoral sexual abuse.[2]

Early in 1992 the Australian Broadcasting Corporation televised a program entitled "The Ultimate Betrayal: Sexual Violence in the Church" (15 March 1992) which sought to highlight the issue of sexual abuse and assault by clergy persons through dramatized recreations of specific events. The events were sensationalized and the issue received national media coverage for a week or so. However in many ways what was presented in the program was not typical. The incidents portrayed had more of the nature of sexual assault. While this is a problem, it is likely that this is not the typical problem, which is a much more common and subtle one.

A better illustration was provided by another event which captured global media attention early in 1992. For several weeks the international media delighted in the disclosures surrounding Bishop Eamon Casey and his "affair" with Ms Anne Murphy, an affair which resulted in the birth of a child. While the media focused on the hypocrisy of a man who had publicly supported celibacy among the clergy and stressed the importance of fathers spending more time with their children, this was not the only issue at stake.

We would like to argue that there are two ways of reading the relationship between Bishop Casey and Ms Murphy. The difference between them and the diverse moral evaluations that result are stark. While society and the churches are familiar with the first reading, the second raises issues which the churches must face with some urgency.

On the first reading, Bishop Casey and Ms Murphy are a pair of star-crossed lovers. He was a man struggling with his celibacy, seeking human warmth and relationship. She was a woman on the rebound, recovering from a divorce, looking for love. It might even have been a case of love at first sight, both falling hopelessly in love with one another. Yet sadly it was a relationship doomed to failure. He was a bishop married to his church, she a divorcee. The impending birth of a child made the hopelessness of their

---

[2] P. Cooper-White, "Soul Stealing: Power Relations in Pastoral Sexual Abuse", *The Christian Century*, 20 February 1991.

situation evident to both of them and the relationship was terminated. It was doomed from the start, a tragic yet romantic chapter in both their lives.

A second reading would see this as a case of pastoral sexual abuse, where a clergyman uses his pastoral power and authority to exploit a vulnerable woman for sexual purposes.

This reading would note that (according to press reports) Ms Murphy was visiting Ireland to recover from what she described as "a messy divorce." She was alone, away from her usual family supports and hurting deeply. She would thus have been highly vulnerable and open to emotional and sexual exploitation. Bishop Casey was a respected public figure carrying religious authority and personal charisma. He was also around twenty years older than Ms Murphy. In the terms analyzed in the introduction, he was clearly the more powerful person in the relationship. The initiation of, or even response to, sexual activity under such circumstances was an abuse of his position for his own sexual ends. Given the differential in power in the relationship, and the position of trust which the Bishop held, it would have been almost impossible for Ms Murphy to reject any approach from him. He could also depend on her to keep his activities secret in order to protect his continuing ministry. Finally his termination of the relationship when his own sexual irresponsibility led to the conception of a child would indicate that he had no significant personal commitment to Ms Murphy or the child she bore, thus adding to the abusiveness of the relationship.

On such a reading, this case would appear to be more typical of sexual abuse by clergy than the type presented by the television program mentioned above. It involves not assault but seduction. The victim gets so drawn into the web of the perpetrator that she may no longer see herself as a victim. Indeed she may experience herself as "madly in love" with the perpetrator, though it is likely that this state was itself the product of the minister's sexual advances, not the cause of them. Yet the differential in power and the lack of committed reciprocity in the relationship defines the situation as one of abuse.

## IS IT A COMMON PROBLEM?

In discussing the issue of pastoral sexual abuse, the first question which is raised is that of rates of incidents. Church spokespersons will often reassure their people that "while, yes, this goes on and is regrettable, it is not a common problem." Of course it is impossible to get precise figures on such matters but there are indications which do give some guidance. For example, it can be noted that despite clear ethical guidelines, one survey of over 1000 psychiatrists in the USA revealed that 7.1 per cent *admitted* to a sexual relationship with some clients. In the medical field, a similar survey of physicians revealed that 13 per cent had some form of sexual involvement with clients, with 80 per cent of these having an average of six victims.[3] Such relationships are professionally abusive.

While in the public perception church ministers will have higher ethical standards than people in secular professions, such is not necessarily the case. In fact given that there are fewer mechanisms for professional accountability for those in ministry, that they have no clear code of professional ethics, and that their training in counseling skills and its complexities is minimal, it would come as no surprise if ministers were to have a worse record than secular professionals.

There is reason to believe that figures for other countries will be at least as high as those gathered in the USA.[4] For example, a document adopted by the General Assembly of the Presbyterian Church (USA) states that:

> statistical evidence suggests between 10 and 23 per cent of clergy
> nationwide have engaged in sexualized behavior or sexual contact
> with parishioners, clients, employees etc, within a professional rela-
> tionship. The toll of suffering such behavior exacts is staggering.[5]

---

[3] See Rutter, op. cit., p.35.
[4] A report in *The Age* (Melbourne, Australia, 17 July 1991, p.3) cited a survey conducted in 1989 by European criminologists that showed significantly higher rates of sexual violence reported in Australia than in the USA, Canada or West Germany.
[5] Cf. "Policies and Procedures on Sexual Misconduct" adopted by the General Assembly of the Presbyterian Church (USA) in 1991.

Further, when the research department of the journal *Christianity Today* surveyed evangelical ministers with the question "Since you've been in local church ministry have you ever done anything with someone (not your spouse) that you feel was sexually inappropriate?", 23 per cent said yes. In response to another question, 12 per cent admitted to having sexual intercourse with someone other than their spouse.[6] Other estimates give similar figures. Conservative author and pastor Tim LaHaye quotes a survey of 300 clergy indicating that 33 per cent of those polled confessed to "sexually inappropriate behavior" with someone other than their spouse; 13 per cent reported that they had had sexual intercourse with a parishioner.[7]

More disturbing still is the fact that typically an offending minister will have multiple victims. A 1990 United Methodist study indicated that of the nearly 1600 individuals surveyed, nearly 23 per cent of laywomen said they had been sexually harassed, 17 per cent by their own pastor and 9 per cent by another minister.[8]

The overall picture which emerges from these surveys is one not dissimilar to that of other helping professions. If anything the figures are higher, though some may say this is simply a case of greater honesty in response to the survey questions!

## THE MINISTER'S POWER AS A PROFESSIONAL

The issues confronting ministers are no different from those facing members of other helping professions, such as teachers, lecturers, counselors, therapists and so on. In many of these professions there are clear ethical guidelines which forbid sexual relationships between the professional person and her or his clients. In his book *Sex in the Forbidden Zone*, Peter Rutter notes that in the USA,

---

[6] Quoted by Jay Jordan-Lake, "Conduct Unbecoming a Preacher", *Christianity Today*, 10 February 1992.

[7] LaHaye, T., *If Ministers Fail, Can They Be Restored?*, (Zondervan Publishing House, 1990).

[8] Cf. "Sexual Harassment in the United Methodist Church", 1990, reported by Jay Jordan-Lake, ibid.

the four major professional groups that account for almost all psychotherapists—psychiatrists (MDs); psychologists (PhDs); social workers (LCSWs): and marriage, family and child counselors—state much the same thing in their own way ... [that] sexual relationships with people under their care are wrong.[9]

In Australia similar restrictions apply in the medical profession, with psychiatry being an area of particular concern. In New Zealand the legal profession has even taken a stand on the issue, claiming that sexual relations with clients constitutes professional sexual abuse. These restrictions are based on the recognition of the manifest disparity in power between the client and the professional, which makes true consent to sexual advances psychologically next to impossible. Despite the stand taken by these secular professions, the churches have been slower to recognize that similar dynamics operate in many pastoral settings. The churches' response to "sexual misconduct" by its ministers has been to see it as not serious, as a problem of mutual responsibility between two consenting adults. There is little if any recognition of the power imbalance in the pastoral setting. In this area the churches have shown less moral sensitivity than the secular professions.

## THE ISSUE OF POWER

It is the issue of power in relationships which gives ministry much in common with other helping professions, and the same ethical standards need to be applied.

Ministers, like other helping professionals, have a constant stream of people seeking their assistance on the most intimate of matters. By virtue of their office they have access to the deepest fears, longings and pains of their congregants. Congregants have the right to expect that the minister will act in a way which is in the congregant's best interest, and the right to be safe from exploitation. Experience indicates that ministers (and others such as therapists, counselors, etc.) who exploit such situations for sexual purposes are in fact never acting in the best interests of the

---

[9] Rutter, p.161.

client, whatever they might think or however they might justify such actions. In fact their actions are severely damaging.

The principle involved is that people in such a vulnerable situation have a diminished ability to refuse the advances of the more powerful person.[10] In some American States such advances by a therapist constitute a criminal offence, where the apparent consent of the client is no defense (it carries a jail term of 5–10 years).[11] Ministers have been willing to use sessions of pastoral counseling, and even sacramental settings, to make sexual advances, claiming, "This is the way I show affection." In the terms of the previously mentioned law, this constitutes a "therapeutic deception." It is a gross violation of the needs and vulnerabilities of the client. Indeed a recent court case led to a $1.2 million judgment against an Episcopalian diocese because of the activities of one of its priests in relation to a woman who had come for counseling, even though the woman may have taken initiatives in the sexual side of the relationship.[12]

Of course added to the abuse which arises in secular situations is the religious significance of the minister. In the Catholic tradition the priest acts *in persona Christi*. As an ordained figure his task is to mediate Christ's love for his church concretely to the Catholic community. He stands as God's representative to God's people and so when he acts in a sexually abusive manner to a woman there are inevitable consequences for her spiritual life and personal development. Protestant authors Lebacqz and Barton argue that Protestant ministers also carry this numinous aspect to their work, with the same consequences when they act it out sexually. They note:

> Because of the authority and the numinous dimension of the pastoral role, it is difficult if not impossible to escape the role ... This numinous dimension of relating the congregation to the divine is

---

[10] For a detailed study of the psychodynamics from a Jungian perspective, see Rutter.

[11] Cf. *Sexual Assault and Abuse: A Handbook for Clergy and Religious Professionals*, M. Pellauer, B. Chester and J. Boyajian (eds), (Harper San Francisco), pp.267–8, Chap.18, n.1.

[12] Cf, *Working Together*, the newsletter for the Center for the Prevention of Sexual and Domestic Violence, Seattle, USA, Vol. 12, No.1, p.10.

clearly linked to the expectations that the pastor be exemplary in moral behavior. It also means that pastors have tremendous power over parishioners ... The power to define a parishioner's status with God is a power that comes with the particular role of minister.[13]

## CONSEQUENCES FOR THE WOMEN

The message women receive in such circumstances is that even God sees them of value only as a sexual object. The minister adds the voice of God to what is commonly a history of self-disesteem and self-blame. The minister's actions can destroy the spiritual life of the woman, making her feel totally unworthy of God's love and forgiveness. Indeed she can feel as if God himself has abused her.

Often women who are so affected drift away from the churches and lose any spiritual sense. This is all the more treacherous given that women will often approach a minister precisely because he offers the hope of some spiritual guidance and insight. Abusive actions therefore are not simply abusive but blasphemous, using God's name in vain. Ministers who act in this way are sacrificing women to their own sexual or other intra-psychic compulsions. In theological terms this involves a negation of the sacrifice of Christ, whose death was once and for all. Rather than furthering the work of Christ, such ministers are in fact undoing the work of Christ. They are literally "de-evangelizing," taking away the Gospel from those they serve through their abusive actions.[14]

There are many ways in which women emerge as the silent victims of pastoral sexual abuse by ministers. There are devastating psychological as well as spiritual consequences for the victims. Given that such abuse is a betrayal of the trust of a vulnerable person by a more powerful one, the psychodynamics are similar to those in a parent–child relationship in which "consent" is the product of emotional coercion. Hence it is not surprising that the effects are often similar to those of incest victims.

---

[13] Lebacqz and Barton, pp.110–111.
[14] We first heard the term "de-evangelization" in regard to pastoral sexual abuse from Rev. Patricia Allen at the "Project Anna" seminar in Melbourne, November 1993.

As if to reinforce the incestuous symbolism, one perpetrator of pastoral sexual abuse, who abused a married women twenty years younger than himself, described his actions as "showing fatherly affection."[15]

While initially the sexual attention may have been experienced as positive and flattering, eventually confusion, loss of self-esteem, self-doubt, anxiety, panic attacks, shame and depression take over. These feelings disorient the victims leaving them unable to trust their own experience, their own feelings. They do not want to believe that the minister was not truly caring. They lose trust in the world and in society. Depression can take over to the point where a victim contemplates suicide.

In these abusive relationships it is emotional coercion rather than physical coercion which is operating. Women report feeling emotionally "tied" to the minister, at its worst to the point of feeling trapped. They invest emotionally in the relationship even if the minister does not. Thus when the relationship ends, especially if the minister terminates it abruptly, victims experience severe grief reactions. Most often victims remain traumatized for years.

Commonly women who have been abused in such situations suffer profound feelings of guilt and shame. They blame themselves, sometimes to the point of completely ignoring the minister's responsibility. They may feel they have led him astray, or that they have betrayed their own marriage partner.

I was a migrant girl, eighteen years old, going on nineteen. Life at home was emotionally arid because my parents took no interest in my social or emotional needs. We were a very achievement-oriented family. Even at that age my mother would slap me in the face as a way of showing disapproval. I lacked any self-esteem and had no real girlfriends, much less boyfriends. I associated my sexuality with shame, but it was something I naturally wanted to explore one day and I certainly wanted to be attractive.

It was at this point in my life that my parents and three younger brothers went away for a week. The senior minister of the parish called around, a man in his mid-forties. I liked him. I saw him as kind and attentive, and of course I welcomed him in.

---

[15] Cf. M. Pellauer et al., p.210.

11

The last thing I expected was that he would be sexual with me. In fact, he was full on. He made a few other "pastoral visits" that week, after which I went to see him, but only occasionally. I wasn't in love with him. It was just that I enjoyed the attention. It wasn't long, though, before the guilt became too much and I stopped seeing him.

Some people in the parish suspected something was going on and it was clear from their behavior they disapproved of me. I felt really out in the cold. One of them shared their suspicions with my parents and they were very angry. What little respect they had ever shown seemed to disappear, especially my mother. She confronted me with it in a public situation, which was humiliating. It created such a rift between us that I had to leave home.

The whole thing has had a profound effect on my life. It put me in such moral turmoil that I was then only comfortable with the thought of sexual intimacy if it was in the context of marriage, and I rushed into marriage with my present husband just one year later. Our marriage was put on the wrong footing from the beginning.

I've never been able to hold my head high since all this happened, over twenty years ago, and I've never really come to grips with it. I so badly compromised my ideal of chastity. Until only a few years ago I saw myself as completely responsible. The woman was supposed to be the strong one. The minister later thanked me for not putting in a complaint. I was shocked because it was the last thing on my mind.

I always blamed myself because I knew it was wrong at the time and I didn't act on that. I think now I didn't stop him because I had no idea what I was giving up—I didn't see myself as valuable anyway. Actually, where I had wondered if I was lovable before that, after it I was convinced I was not.

Only in recent years have I begun to think the minister bore some responsibility for what happened, in spite of the fact that my husband has always been angry with him. And the concept of him having responsibility because he was my pastor is still new to me. I'm beginning to realize he should have protected me. And yet I'm still not able to get angry.

In the long term, damage can include nightmares, chronic depression, dissociation from feelings and social withdrawal due

12

to profound loss of self-esteem and trust. Many of these effects are those associated with post-traumatic stress disorder.[16]

Then there are the more tangible consequences for some women, such as for Anne Murphy. Unplanned pregnancies mean painful decisions about whether to raise the child alone, have the child adopted out or terminate the pregnancy. Ministers have been known to put pressure on the woman about what should happen, including pressure to have a termination.[17] The consequences of such decisions are life-long.

Other relationships may also be affected. Some victims report a diminished ability to respond sexually to more appropriate

---

[16] See Mollie Brown, "From Victim to Survivor: The Treatment of Adults who have been Sexually Abused as Children", *Slayer of the Soul*, p.85. She lists the following criteria for the disorder:

"1. The person has experienced an event that is outside the range of usual human experience and that would be markedly distressing to almost anyone.

2. The traumatic event is persistently re-experienced in at least one of the following ways: a) recurrent and intrusive recollections of the event; b) recurrent distressing dreams of the event; c) sudden acting or feeling as if the traumatic event were recurring ...; d) intense psychological distress at exposure to events that symbolize or represent an aspect of the traumatic event, including anniversaries of the trauma.

3. Persistent avoidance of stimuli associated with the trauma or numbing of general responsiveness ... as indicated by the following: a) efforts to avoid thoughts or feelings associated with the trauma; b) efforts to avoid activities or situations that arouse recollections of the trauma; c) inability to recall an important aspect of the trauma ...; d) markedly diminished interest in significant activities ...; e) feeling of detachment or estrangement from others; f) restricted sense of affect; g) sense of foreshortened future ...

4. Persistent symptoms of increased arousal ... as indicated by at least two of the following: a) difficulty in falling asleep; b) irritability or outbursts of anger; c) difficulty concentrating; d) hypervigilance; e) exaggerated startle response; f) physiologic reactivity upon exposure to events which symbolize or resemble an aspect of the traumatic event."

We have listed this in detail as an aid to survivors in identifying their own experience of abuse. We have seen all these symptoms in survivors of pastoral sexual abuse.

[17] Priests in such situations have been known to ask the woman to have an abortion, cf. the case of Fr Chris O'Neill, *The Tablet*, 5 September 1992, p.1115.

partners. If a woman is married and her husband finds out, their marriage may break up. The woman may find herself vulnerable to other exploitative relationships because of the damage done to her personal boundaries. It is not uncommon to find women who are victims of multiple abuse. The necessary secrecy is usually felt to be extremely isolating and oppressive. If the victim does disclose to other members of her church congregation she will usually experience re-victimization. There will be those who don't believe her, or who will blame her for being a seductress. Usually she loses her faith community because she can no longer feel safe there. For a woman whose church was part of her support network this blow can be devastating.

Eventually the victim of these experiences must either deny the importance of them in her life or must come to terms with them. The healing process is itself arduous and can take years. Anger at the betrayal of trust is often the first sign that the victim is moving towards being a survivor.[18]

The following was written by a survivor who heard that one priest had asked, "Is it really all that damaging?"

> When I was in my mid-thirties and looking for who I was and a deeper spiritual awareness I turned for help to a priest who was also a counselor, lecturer and friend. Instead of support in confronting my problems he initiated a sexual relationship, then rejected me. Disaster followed.
>
> When the inner turmoil became too great I told my husband about the relationship, resulting in a total breakdown of my mental health and four weeks in a private psychiatric hospital.
>
> The pain and fear was total. I did not know how I would stay in existence with the terrible pain enveloping my total being. Only God would keep me there, stopping me from ceasing to exist.
>
> The wound in my mind and spirit about the relationship with this priest was horrendous. I struggled for ten years with the pain, shame and wound, seeing a psychiatrist almost ninety times in this period and taking anti-depressants and other medication.
>
> It was only by the power of God at a healing Mass, that God's love healed the terrible wound in my mind and spirit, and gave me

---

[18] This is taken up in greater detail in Chapter Three.

14

again the will to live and also the motivation to lose the 22 kilograms I gained during this period.

My husband in turn had to cope with a wife who was not an adult partner but an emotional and sexual cripple, who was heavily dependent upon him to cope with family and life in general. I thank both God and my husband for my husband's great love and inner strength. He had always said the priest was fully responsible for the relationship, but I could never understand my emotional tie and spiritual involvement with this priest.

It was only some twelve years later while I was still searching for the cause of my problems that the pieces of the jigsaw finally began fitting together. I was going to women only for counseling when I regained the memories of being sexually abused by my grandfather who was a doctor and pillar of the church.

The abuse began when I was only two years old and continued for many years. It was all blocked out for forty-six years, but I now have finally found the cause of my fear—*The secret.*

As an adult when I was searching for a way out of the suppressed fear and pain I turned to someone who represented God, who had always been my one lifeline. This priest, being a counselor, had the knowledge to help me. I knew this and gave myself in trust to him for a way out of the fog. Instead of helping me face my fear, he in turn emotionally manipulated and sexually abused me. I had been programmed by earlier abuse, which had damaged my boundaries, to be open to sexual abuse.

By telling my husband of this adult "secret" I blew all my fuses for I had been programmed by my grandfather that if I told "the secret" I would lose everything.

So instead of having only my childhood abuse still to be dealt with—which was prevented from happening for years—I also had the adult abuse.

All this has also left me for years with a sense of loss, of no longer belonging to a church and community. I have no trouble with God as He has always been my lifeline and friend. But the hypocrisy and abusive power of the church makes me feel very angry and distressed. I can't even go to Mass because the stress causes such nausea after five minutes at Mass that I want to vomit.

Who said "Is it really all that damaging?"

## THE MORAL DIMENSION

The other silent victim is the minister's own conscience. Firstly, he must rationalize his departure from his freely undertaken vow of celibacy or his own marriage vows, with consequent distortion of his conscience. Secondly, there is the more significant failure to recognize the consequences of his actions in relationship to another person, the woman involved. What could have been an opportunity for real personal growth leads instead to a deadening of conscience which can make further abusive relationships with other women even more likely. Indeed, in our experience, multiple abusive relationships appears to be part of the pattern of pastoral sexual abuse, as in other helping professions.

In an as-yet-unpublished article, the noted author and theologian, Sebastian Moore picks up the nature of this failure in reference to the life of St Augustine. He notes that:

> ... at a turning-point of his life, Augustine allowed his mother to dismiss his common-law wife! This is perhaps the most serious sexual sin in his life, a sin against the spousal nature of sex, and of it he shows no sign of needing to repent. On the contrary he sees the dismissal as a vital step towards God. The ending of this marriage—the woman's name is not even mentioned—is presented as the ending of a bad habit.[19]

Sexual relationships with women are not bad habits, indulgences, or little weaknesses. They involve real people. Failure to grasp the significance of such relationships and their effects upon the women involved represents a serious moral failure on the part of the minister.

Beyond the interpersonal dimensions lies the broader social context. The moral theorist Alasdair MacIntyre has argued that any community which is constituted by a shared project, such as a Christian community, will recognize two types of moral precepts.

> On the one hand they would need to value ... those qualities of mind and character which would contribute to the realization of

---

[19] S. Moore, "The Bedded Axle Tree", MS, p.8, 5 May 1992.

their common goods. That is they would need to recognize a certain set of qualities as virtues and the corresponding set of defects
as vices … They would also need however to identify certain types
of action as the doing or production of harm of such an order that
they destroy the bonds of community in such a way as to render
the doing or the producing of good impossible in some respect …
The response to such offences would have to be that of taking the
person who committed them to have thereby excluded himself or
herself from the community.[20]

Too often the perception of the churches and its ministers is
that the sexual misconduct of its ministers is just a failure of virtue,
a lapse from the high ideal of Christian morality, a morality which
holds equally for all Christians. It is the basic position of this work
that such sexual misconduct is, rather, a failure against an absolute
precept, one which is sufficiently intolerable to exclude the
minister involved from the community and certainly from the
further exercise of ministry, until such time as proper restitution is
made. It is a betrayal of the whole community.

In justice, ministers must acknowledge that they are in positions of trust, responsibility and power in relationship to their
clients. Through their ordination the community invests them with
a power corresponding to the leadership role they play in the
community. People come to them precisely because of the power
and authority that ministers have in relation to spiritual matters.
This power brings with it corresponding responsibilities for them
to act in the best interests of those who come seeking help. The
church community invests its trust in ministers that they will use
the power that they have to act in a responsible manner. When
ministers abuse their position for a sexual end they not only
severely affect the spiritual and personal development of the
women involved, they also undermine the antecedent trust in the
ministry itself. Without such trust the leadership role of the
minister becomes empty and meaningless.

---

[20] Cf. Alasdair MacIntyre, *After Virtue*, (Notre Dame; University of Notre Dame
Press, 2nd ed, 1984), p.151.

## ARE THERE ANY EXCEPTIONS?

So far this analysis has focused on relationships between ministers and women in their pastoral care and highlighted the ways in which this can be abusive of the women involved. One should also note the possibility of ministers entering into homosexual relationships with men in their pastoral care. Inasmuch as the same analysis holds, this is a serious abuse of the minister's role. Moreover, it carries with it the extra stigma of the activities involved, which many Christian groups regard as being immoral, so that the pressure to maintain secrecy will be greater.

One should also acknowledge that some ministers do enter into sexual relationships with women (and men) outside their pastoral sphere, friends from before the time of their own ordination or people not connected with their church. It may be possible for such relationships to be non-abusive, with a clear negotiation of mutual expectations and limits. The evaluation of such relationships in terms of sexual morality is beyond the scope of this book. All that we note here is that such activity may not involve an abuse of the minister's pastoral role. It should be noted, of course, that in Protestant circles a minister has a right to court and marry, and so all such relationships cannot be ruled out.

However Catholic priests may find it difficult to circumscribe the limits of their pastoral responsibilities and great caution needs to be exercised. The question which may be asked is, "When is a priest not a priest?" Here the Catholic tradition speaks of priesthood as grounded in an ontological, not just a functional reality. The priest does not cease being a priest because he moves out of his normal ministerial situation or takes off his collar. People may have expectations of him as a priest even though he feels he is not acting as a minister. His situation is determined not just by his desire for time off, but also by the expectations of the person to whom he relates.

Now this discussion may seem foreign to those outside the Catholic tradition, but the general structure is not. A Protestant minister who is married has as much, if not more, reason than a celibate priest to not engage in sexual activity with those in his pastoral care. Such activity would violate his marriage vows.

Protestant authors are beginning to question whether it is ethical for an unmarried minister to marry someone in his congregation.[21] Finally, the Orthodox tradition, while it has allowed married men into ministry, does not allow those who have entered ministry as single men to marry. As in the Catholic tradition, they remain celibate. Perhaps in this way their tradition recognizes that entry into ministry changes the ways in which it is permissible for a minister to relate to his congregation. The celibacy of the minister is then a way of honoring those in his pastoral care, of seeking to protect them from sexual exploitation, by establishing clear boundaries around the minister.[22]

## CONCLUSION

In handling this whole issue, the churches are facing important pastoral and moral problems. Sexual abuse undermines the churches' moral authority and calls into question its pastoral practices, not just in the original abuse but in the ways in which disclosures of abuse are handled. At the communal level the churches could face a major crisis of confidence in its ministers. Ministers who act out sexually have undermined their moral authority when it comes to speaking on issues of sexual morality. Their abuse of particular women becomes an abuse of the whole community as it ties them into patterns of deceit and secrecy. The trust of the whole community is violated. These are some of the issues we shall explore in the following chapters.

---

[21] Though Lebacqz and Barton note the restrictions which are operative even for Protestant ministers, pp.172–191.
[22] Perhaps here we can see the link, stressed by Pope John Paul II, between ministry and celibacy. We take this up again in the next chapter.

# CHAPTER TWO

# CELIBACY: PROBLEM

# OR SOLUTION?

I n a Catholic context no discussion of the issue of sexual abuse can take place without some reference to the issue of celibacy. Indeed for a scandal-hungry media celibacy is often the sole explanation for the sexual-abusive actions of priests, while Catholic church authorities will forcefully deny any link. Any reflection at all upon the question of sexual abuse makes it clear that celibacy is not the cause, since married Protestant ministers are implicated as well. To focus on celibacy as the cause is to see sexual abuse as a problem of sexual aberration, whereas the key issues are those of power and ministerial responsibility.

However it cannot be denied that there is some interaction of the two issues of abuse and celibacy. On the one hand the institutional imposition of celibacy can invoke considerable sympathy from people in general, including potential victims. Certainly some priests are not above exploiting such sympathy for their own sexual purposes. People can feel sorry for priests because of the burden of celibacy. They may excuse their sexual "indiscretions" as understandable and perhaps even tolerable. Certainly among their fellow priests there is evidence of a culture of tolerance towards sexual misconduct—the sin is not in the misconduct, but in being caught with your pants down!

Further it must be acknowledged that priests can have an honest struggle to come to grips with their celibacy as they experience all the normal human biological urges and fantasies which are part of a normal male's existence. There may also be mourning for the lost opportunities for fatherhood and the likelihood of loneliness in old age to contend with. We also have a culture which tends to both glorify and minimize the significance of casual sexual activity. All these things make celibacy difficult to maintain.

On the other hand public exposure of the sexual activity of a priest carries with it the shame of violated vows, hypocrisy and damage to the reputation of the church. None of these are light matters.

Clearly seminary formation in celibacy is essential for the prospective priest to be able to come to a responsible decision about his future. Moreover Catholic church authorities and communities have a right to expect that those who enter ministry will behave in a responsible manner with regard to their vow of celibacy. If these authorities or communities find that this is not the case then they must question the ongoing suitability of the person for ministry. If a priest finds he can no longer live in a celibate manner he must also act responsibly and question his ongoing commitment to ministry.

This is not a question of supporting or rejecting the present Catholic link between ministry and celibacy. In fact later in this chapter we shall be arguing for the positive significance of celibacy in ministry. Rather it is a recognition that people must act responsibly within the structures that exist and to which they have freely committed themselves. The alternative is self-deception, public damage to the church and inevitable abuse of the women involved.

An example of a failure to take responsibility comes from one survivor of pastoral sexual abuse. The priest who abused her said on one occasion, with some pleasure, "I'm really fortunate that I can have sexual intimacy with a woman without the responsibilities that normally go with it, and also have the fulfillment that goes with my ministry. I get the best of both worlds." When exposed he, and others, excused his multiple abusive activities as "naïvety."

Self-deception occurs when a priest rationalizes his behavior by minimizing the significance of what he is doing. The common and widespread popular rejection of the link between celibacy and ministry makes it easy to justify his own individual violation of his vow. Yet a far more dangerous minimization occurs concerning the nature of the relationship involved. In minimizing his actions the priest also minimizes the relationship with the woman towards whom he is being sexual. Sexual behavior has its own inner dynamic which the Christian tradition sees as heading towards committed, permanent union in marriage. At a social and cultural level it is expressive of courtship and mating. At the moral level it is expressive of committed exclusive relationship.

For a celibate to initiate or respond to sexual behavior is to begin to make promises, though unspoken, which he may have no intention of keeping. Women are real people with real hopes, needs and expectations. A priest who enters into a sexual relationship with a woman under his pastoral care must ask himself: "Is this woman more important to me than my ministry?" If the answer is no, then he must terminate the relationship, since in truth he is simply using her for his own ends.

Some rationalizations we have heard are the following: "Of all our weaknesses, we need feel least remorseful about our sexual sins since they are simply about human frailty"; "This is how I show affection"; "I need to explore my sexuality."

Priests in such situations find themselves separating out their private from their public roles. The relationship becomes not just a private matter but a secret matter. Public knowledge about the nature of the relationship must be kept secret so that the priest can maintain his ministry. The woman involved is subordinated to the requirement of celibacy in ministry and such a situation is invariably abusive of the woman. The expression of her needs, feelings and rights must be kept from public sight lest the priest be exposed.

Anna came to her new parish hurting deeply. She was unemployed, lonely and in an unsatisfactory housing arrangement. From a childhood of severe emotional and physical abuse she had gone into a violent marriage, ending in divorce. She then fell into a year-long sexual relationship with a priest which the priest had both initiated and ended suddenly.

The parish priest in the new parish visited Anna regularly. Anna found him very supportive but before long the relationship became sexualized. He invited her to be housekeeper at the presbytery. Anna was infatuated with him and agreed, pleased to be asked.

However she quickly found the secrecy of the sexual relationship oppressive. There was no-one in whom she could confide if they were in conflict over something. She knew that his status meant that parishioners would look favorably on him and see her as a loose woman.

The fact that she was living in the presbytery had to be kept secret also. Anna was expected on occasion to remain in her bedroom for hours at a time, perfectly quiet, because he had visitors. She was not even allowed to cough, which was difficult at times for an asthmatic.

Over time he became increasingly emotionally abusive towards her. He blamed her for everything that was going wrong in the relationship. On two occasions he locked her out of the presbytery while she was still in her pyjamas. She had no-one to turn to and on both occasions became hysterical.

Finally Anna left the presbytery, but the relationship continued for some years. He often impressed on her the importance of not telling anyone about the closeness of their relationship. Anna always had to be careful not to ring the presbytery too often. At the same time he would not exclude the possibility of a future committed relationship.

Anna became increasingly impatient with the fact that he treated their relationship as such a poor second priority to his parish duties. But there was no-one with whom to talk about it and feel confident of some acceptance. And of course relationship counseling was out of the question. She became thoroughly disillusioned with the Catholic faith.

Eventually Anna died of breast cancer. Was this a consequence of her lifetime of abuse?

Given the privileged and high status position of the priest in the community, the woman can find herself with no-one to share her plight, no-one to counsel her and no avenues for redress when wronged. Indeed she is likely to be blamed for "leading the priest astray." There are also the more tangible prices to pay, as we discussed in the last chapter. The fact that women may seem willing to pay such a price in a relationship is more a function of patterns of abuse of females which are so prevalent in society.[1] To exploit such a willingness is an exploitation of another's vulnerability and as such is abusive.

## COMMON RATIONALIZATIONS

The issue of celibacy is a rich source of rationalizations for priests who wish to engage in pastoral sexual abuse. In researching this book we have come across a number of such rationalizations, which priests use to justify their sexual activities. We would now like to deal with these explicitly to uncover their dangers and inadequacies.

### * Priests have a need for intimacy

It can be argued that everyone has a need for intimacy and priests, like everyone else, need to find appropriate ways of fulfilling that need. Like many a rationalization, this contains a half-truth. The full development of our human personality requires intimate relationship with other persons. There is no need, however, that this be expressed in a sexual manner. Also our human need is not a need for intimacy *per se*, but intimate *relationship*. A priest who seeks to satisfy his "need for intimacy" by relating to one or more women in a sexual manner, may not in fact be meeting his real need for intimate *relationship*. He may simply be using the women as a means to an end, rather than relating in real mutuality and interdependence. Then a sexual relationship becomes a shield to prevent real intimacy, an alternative to real vulnerability and sharing. This constitutes an abuse.

### * This is how I show affection

This rationalization deludes the priest into making his action seem selfless, that he is doing the woman a favor, when in fact he is far more likely to be operating out of his own unacknowledged needs rather than the needs of the woman. Such a rationalization

---

[1] Research indicates that up to 38 per cent of women experience some form of sexual assault or abuse before the age of 18, cf. D. Finkelnor, *Sexually Victimized Children*, (New York; Free Press, 1979) (referred to in a paper by Peter Horsfield, "Is the Dam of Sexual Assault Breaking in the Church?", *Australian Ministry*, May, 1992).

becomes just a form of self-deception. Similarly some priests argue that in a difficult pastoral situation, it's better to love more than less. Rather than back away and love less, it may be better to love more and this may involve getting sexually involved with a woman. Again this sounds an attractive rationalization but it ignores several things. A father, for example, must love his daughter more, rather than less, but this can never justify an incestuous relationship. Given the damage that can often be done to women in pastoral situations, it is not more loving to become sexually involved, rather it is more loving, more respectful, to refrain from sexual involvement and maintain clear sexual boundaries.

### * It's not sexual unless it's genital

Some priests engage in sexual activity but rationalize it on the grounds that it does not become full genital intercourse. They restrict their activities to what might be termed "heavy petting." There are three problems with this. Firstly, such activity is socially identified with courtship and mating. For a priest to engage in such activity is to send out mixed messages to women about his commitment to celibacy and thus his ministry. As such it can deceive a woman about the nature of the relationship. Secondly, it fails radically to take into account the significance and effect of such activity on the woman involved. Such activity can elicit quite a powerful response from the woman, to the extent of hampering her sexual response in other, more legitimate relationships. Thirdly, it sets up situations where one of the two will get "carried away" and intercourse will occur. The possibility of unplanned and unwanted pregnancy is not far away. It is irresponsible to act in this way.

One should also note that some priests who engage in abuse of children, particularly male children, do not see their activity as acting against their celibacy. Only activity with women is thought of as sexual.[2] Such men are not homosexual,[3] and are attracted to women, but they see that as incompatible with their celibacy. This denial about pedophilia is indicative of the depth of rationalization that can occur.

---

[2] Cf. S. Rossetti and L. Lothstein, "Myths of the Child Molester", in S. Rossetti, *Slayer of the Soul*, p.13.

[3] It is a too common mistake to confuse pedophilia with adult homosexuality.

## * Women throw themselves at ministers

Clergy often note the problem of having women throw themselves at them. Marie Fortune notes:

> Whenever the issue of clergy sexual contact with parishioners arises, the most common concern of clergy is to express their need to be protected from seductive, manipulative parishioners.[4]

It becomes difficult to resist such temptation, and it seems to them that it really is the woman's fault. It is important here for ministers to understand the psychological dynamics of such actions. The problem of "women throwing themselves at us" is commonly voiced by many in the helping professions. Its cause is not the uncommon attractiveness of ministers and other professionals but more a very common form of psychological brokenness among the women concerned. Women who have suffered from sexual abuse as children have been taught that their only value to a man is as a sexual object. Other forms of physical and psychological abuse and neglect can lead women to seek affirmation from a father-figure. "Throwing themselves" at men in powerful positions (as father substitutes) may be a desperate plea to receive affirmation in the only way that they know how.

To refuse such activity, yet remain affirming and supportive, can be a real healing moment for the woman. To exploit such vulnerability constitutes a further abuse in the woman's existing history of sexual or psychological abuse. It becomes the psychological equivalent of incest.

On the other side of the coin the impression of "women throwing themselves" at ministers may be a matter of simple projection. Where a male minister is not aware of his own psychic processes, where he represses or denies his own sexuality, then projection is a real danger. Such repression and denial appear to be common among celibates, as a coping mechanism. Abusive persons can even project their own sexual desires onto children, let alone an adult woman. Before making claims about women "throwing themselves" at ministers, the ministers must address

---

[4] Fortune, p.121.

their own psychological processes and become more sensitive to their own responses.

*Married women are safer, they're less likely to become attached*

The most frightening attitude we have heard in researching this book is, "If you are going to get involved with a woman, it's better if she is married, she'll be less apt to cling to you." While this may have been an individual priest's rationalization of his own behavior, he cited it as "common wisdom" among priests. If true it would indicate a subculture which is willing not only to violate celibacy, but also the sacred bonds of marriage. Particularly vulnerable are women who are experiencing difficulties in their marriages (as all do at some time). There is evidence of priests who have been willing to turn counseling sessions about marriage difficulties to their own sexual advantage. This is clearly abusive.

## CELIBACY AND MINISTRY

Until the Second Vatican Council, celibacy was the unquestioned norm of ministry in the Latin rite of the Catholic Church. However as with many aspects of Catholic life at that time, it was questioned and scrutinized, so that, while the church continued to maintain its discipline of celibacy, the rationale for this discipline became less and less clear. It was pointed out that Scripture presupposes that ministers in the early church were married (cf. I Tim 3:2). Historical studies clarified the processes and motivations behind the adoption of celibacy in ministry, putting them into a new perspective. More generally, people saw celibacy as a denigration of sexuality and hence as anti-human. Increasingly the church has been under pressure to review its compulsory discipline of celibacy, especially since many priests have been leaving ministry to get married.

This institutional uncertainty is not a good atmosphere for men who are seeking to maintain their celibacy. Past rationales no longer seem to make sense and church authorities have not been able to come up with other, more convincing, arguments. Without clear motivations, the Catholic position on celibacy seems like nothing more than an arbitrary imposition whose real but covert rationale is that sex is somehow bad.

There are two key rationales which are put forward as motivation for the church's discipline of celibacy. The first sees celibacy in terms of a greater availability for ministry. A single person is in a better position to "spend himself/herself for the Kingdom." Priests are seen as "eunuchs for the sake of the Kingdom" (cf. Matthew 19:12), following the example of Jesus' own celibacy as a symbol of total commitment to their calling. The second sees celibacy in terms of a spirituality of personal integrity, of pureness of heart, of the proper ordering of human desires undisturbed by sexual passion.

The problem with both of these rationales is that they do not provide grounds for an absolute prohibition of sexual relationships in the setting of ministry. The first rationale does not prohibit sexual relationships *per se*, rather it prohibits committed permanent relationships, since it is marriage which would make the priest "less available." Less permanent, more casual relationships do not undermine this rationale, indeed this rationale may even encourage them, though they may still be seen as "sexual sins," regrettable but not against ministry. This impression is reinforced by the response of the Catholic Church to the sexual activity of its priests. Priests who seek sexual relationship in the permanent bond of marriage, in conformity with the Christian tradition, are excluded from ministry permanently. Those who sexually abuse people in their pastoral care can be "rehabilitated" and returned to ministry. Given this response, marriage is seen institutionally as a more serious "sin" against ministry than sexual abuse! This could well be the message priests are hearing from Catholic Church policies in these matters.

The second rationale has its proper place in Christian spirituality, but has no intrinsic connection to ministry. Again failures in this regard are seen as failures in the virtue of chastity, regrettable but not against ministry.

What is needed is a motivation for celibacy which makes it clear that any sexual activity in a ministerial setting is not consistent with the nature of ministry. If we settle for anything less than this, then we may find that celibacy becomes simply another rationalization for pastoral sexual abuse. To provide such a motivation we shall consider the celibacy of Jesus.

## THE CELIBACY OF JESUS

The ministry of Jesus was one of reaching out to those at the margins of society, the poor, the sick, the broken people. One of the striking personal features of Jesus' ministry was his commitment to celibacy. Unlike the Jewish rabbis of his day, Jesus did not marry, nor is there any indication of his having a sexual relationship with any person (most would see Jesus' sinlessness as excluding non-marital sexual relationships). Another striking feature was his freedom in relationship to women, even women normally excluded from proper religious life: prostitutes, women ritually unclean or in abnormal marriage situations. At a time when an orthodox Jewish man thanked God he was not born a woman and women were forbidden from learning the Torah, Jesus included women in his circle of disciples and welcomed their ministrations.

It is difficult, of course, to get into the mind of Jesus but perhaps we can begin to understand his commitment to celibacy in terms of Jesus' willingness to reach out to women as a religiously and socially marginalized group. Jesus would have understood the exploitative nature of many human sexual relationships. He would have understood the vulnerability of women to sexual exploitation and have had some idea of the high incidence of exploitation in his own society. He would have also sensed his own power in relationship to others and how easy it would have been to exploit that power by manipulating others for his own ends. Perhaps, rather than see Jesus' celibacy as a question of "freedom for the Kingdom" or of "personal integrity" we need to see it as a symbolic statement against the sexual exploitation of women, a way of respecting their vulnerability. Jesus' celibacy created a "safe space" where women were freed from the pressures and fears of sexual abuse.

What is significant about this rationale is that it does not allow for the sexualization of any relationship, for any such action would break the symbolic significance of Jesus' celibacy. Women would no longer be able to feel "safe" in his presence.

If this is an appropriate way to see the celibacy of Jesus then it would seem to indicate that the only coherent approach to celibacy in ministry is that of the Orthodox churches. The Orthodox ordain married men, men who are already in a committed sexual relationship, "a husband of one wife," as Scripture puts it (for example, I Tim 3:2)[5] which should preclude (in principle) any further sexualizing of relationships with women. On the other hand, single men who are ordained remain celibate. This could be seen as a recognition that their relationship to the whole community has changed, in such a way that any sexualizing of a pastoral relationship is forbidden.

If this is indeed the rationale for Jesus' celibacy, then far from being the cause of sexual abuse, celibacy, as it should be lived, is the solution, for the discipline of sexual restraint creates a safe place where women can experience the fullness of God's love, free from the fear of sexual exploitation.

## CONCLUSION

The vow of celibacy taken by priests has meant that the issue of sexual abuse has not received the attention it deserves in the seminary and on-going formation of priests. It is significant to note that none of the key books written on the area of pastoral sexual abuse comes out of a Catholic perspective. On the other hand there are several books by Catholic authors (typically priests) on the issue of celibacy. Peter Rutter notes:

> If one has taken an oath not to have sexual relations of any kind, it may be seen as superfluous to specify that a clergyman must not have sex with a parishioner. As one priest told me, "The Church's position seems to be that since we can't do it at all, there is no point in telling us *with whom* we can't do it."[6]

Such a stance is no longer satisfactory. As with many issues in the Catholic Church, the issue of priestly celibacy is being re-evaluated

---

[5] This is often translated as "only married once," but in fact it denotes more than this, that the marriage commitment is faithful and loving, cf. Edward Schillebeeckx, *The Church with a Human Face*, (London; SCM, 1985) p.240.
[6] Cf. Rutter, p.162.

and re-interpreted. Clearly priests are not asexual beings. However, equally clearly, they need to act with personal and professional responsibility if they are not to find themselves in situations which are inherently abusive of women to whom they may relate. If not they will undermine both their own consciences and the continued moral authority of the church. Seeking to "explore their sexuality" with women for whom they have pastoral responsibility is never the answer.

# CHAPTER THREE

# FROM VICTIM
## TO SURVIVOR

An opinion commonly voiced by church ministers is that, "Yes, abuse goes on, but it's not really damaging." Yet not only is the initial abuse damaging, often leaving life-long scars, but also the process of recovery is itself traumatic, as victims seek to come to grips with what has happened to them. It is in this setting that they may experience what amounts to a second round of abuse from church officials. We shall now explore more closely the process of moving out of being a victim to becoming a survivor.

## WHO ARE THE VICTIMS?

Anyone can become a victim of sexual abuse by their minister. Given the combined circumstances of vulnerability on the part of the victim and the necessary power, always structural and maybe even physical, on the part of the minister, then abuse can occur. Victims can be male or female, old or young, rich or poor, abuse recognizes no barriers, excludes no-one. Vulnerability to abuse may be due to a temporary crisis, such as the death of a child or marriage problems, it may be the result of a previous history of abuse which has blurred one's personal boundaries and made one susceptible, or it may lie simply in the differential of power which exists between the person and their minister. Abuse may take the form of assault or it may be simple seduction, the slower wearing down of sexual boundaries over time. Whatever the circumstances, the vulnerability of the victim has not been respected, rather it has been exploited.

People are not responsible for their vulnerabilities. It is a perversion of logic, a classical case of blaming the victim, to imply that vulnerability is "the cause" of abuse. Vulnerability is the setting in which abuse can take place, but it is not the cause. The cause of abuse is the failure of the abuser to respect that vulnerability, either deliberately or through sheer inattention, through neglect. It is most distressing when ministers abuse precisely because their ministerial task is to respect and protect vulnerability. Of course, the greater the vulnerability, the greater the trust which is placed in the minister and hence the greater the damage done when the minister abuses that trust.

> One woman who had been a victim of childhood abuse, went to a church official to make a disclosure of her past suffering. After confronting the perpetrator, who eventually admitted his actions, the official told her: "Your problem was that you were looking for love in all the wrong places."

Becoming a victim of abuse is a shattering experience. It undermines one's self-esteem, one's sense of one's own dignity. It creates a burden of guilt and shame, guilt at the internalized sense that somehow one is to blame, shame at the thought of what one has endured and what people would say if they knew. Often it shatters one's personal boundaries leaving one vulnerable to further abusive relationships. It is not uncommon to find people who are victims of multiple abuse. It disorients the victims leaving them unable to trust their own experiences, their own feelings. Their most basic trust in others has often been violated.

Finally, when the abuser is a minister, the victims suffer not just from a human betrayal of trust, but betrayal of a sacred trust. The minister is God's agent and carries a "numinous power." When they abuse, it can seem to the victim that it is God who is the ultimate abuser. Their abuse has divine sanction, performed by God's agent. Abuse can shatter the victim's spirituality, the sense of the divine. It raises for the victim ultimate questions about who God is and where God stands. These are all issues which must be dealt with as the victims shed their victimhood and become survivors.

CALLING THE CHILD FROM THE TOMB

I came seeking sanctuary, loving father I never had.
I sought to touch the hem of your garment,
to light the smouldering wick on your Paschal flame.

But your flame set alight something deep inside.
In one hit it flattered and shamed.
A small voice protested,
talked down by your assurances,
too much to lose by resistance.

With you, on a high
flying as on eagles' wings.

Without you, hanging in space,
unacknowledged, unnerved,
fell into despair and out of grace ...
to come back for another hit.

You the innocent, pure and strong,
celibacy comforted.

Me the guilty, weak and wrong,
losing all my sense of God.

Felt compelled to secrecy,
cancer in all intimacy,
invisible wall growing around,
seed over death growing inside,
smothering the inner child.

For years I was driven, deadened,
then came to be drained, wandering.

'Til the prophets named the sin,
called the child forth from the tomb,
to be again with Mother God,
comforter, revitalizing, flood of feeling rising,
strength to smash the walls that hemmed me in.
I reject your hold,
claim my right, my life again.

## FROM VICTIM TO SURVIVOR

Many survivors have experienced within themselves a definite
movement whereby they begin to come to grips with their past

experience of abuse. They begin to recognize that they were not responsible for being abused, that what happened to them was wrong and inexcusable. Paradoxically they can begin to take responsibility for their present life precisely in disclaiming responsibility for their past sufferings—they did not deserve it, it was not a just or divine punishment, they were victims of abuse by another person. Often the difficulty in such an admission is the painful realization of just how little control the victim had in the abusive relationship, often even a reliving of that pain which had been dulled by a misplaced sense of past guilt. Yet in acknowledging their previous experience of being victims of abuse people can begin to break out of the chains of victimhood. They are no longer victims, but are becoming survivors, who begin to reclaim their dignity, their strength and their self-esteem. The spiritual writer John Dunne speaks of this as a movement out of "the hell of the night of private suffering, the suffering of isolation and victimization" and towards the "the suffering of the night of compassion and forgiveness".[1]

Such a movement is not simple or without cost. It will involve a struggle with the twin monsters of guilt and shame, often deeply internalized forces (especially in women) which will attempt to force the survivor back into being a victim. It may mean confronting repressed pain and unleashed anger, struggling with despair, and coming to grips with the issue of forgiving the perpetrator. In all this there will be forces both internal and external which will try to restore the status quo, which will attempt to turn the tide of grace and call into question the validity of the survivor's new interpretation of the past. Survivors are typically told to leave the past behind, stop blaming other people for their problems and get on with their lives. If only the healing process were that simple.

## THE ROLE OF ANGER

Anger is not nice. Anger, we are told by the tradition, is one of the seven deadly sins. In general one would have to say that anger gets a bad press. Nowhere is this more the case than in the

---

[1] John Dunne, *The Way of All the Earth*, (NY; Macmillan, 1972) cited in Robert Doran, *Theology and the Dialectics of History*, (Toronto; University of Toronto Press, 1990), p.114.

churches where it sometimes seems as if anger from the survivor is a more serious sin than the abuse of the perpetrator! Yet like it or not, anger is one thing that a survivor will inevitably feel—anger at the pain of abuse, at having been out of control, at feelings of shame and guilt needlessly imposed by another's actions, at the wasted years as a victim, at the lack of justice offered by church authorities, at the denials of responsibility by the abuser.

Such anger is not just inevitable, it is necessary and good. What happened was wrong and unjust. The survivor has a perfect right to be angry. Indeed it is a sign of grace, a sign of the growing sense of self-worth, which proclaims "I deserved better than this in the past, I deserve better than this now." It is a righteous anger which rejects evil done, rejects it in the name of justice and truth. It is the anger of the prophets when they denounced exploitation of the poor, and Jesus when he cleared the Temple. A survivor of child sexual abuse, Janet Pais, states:

> There is an anger that feels strong and healing. This anger is the energy of expansion after we have been shrunk into less, or distorted into other, than our true selves.[2]

Again there are forces both internal and external which will invalidate the survivor's experience of anger. Internally survivors, particularly women, will feel that such anger is wrong or sinful. They have been told for so long that anger is wrong, they have suppressed it for so long, that they can feel unable to allow it into consciousness. To be angry is bad so they will not allow themselves to feel it.

Externally other voices will join the internal voices, telling them that they should hurry up and get over their anger. Even counselors, who should know better, can be put off by anger or, worse still, tell the survivor that she is being vindictive or unreasonable. Alice Miller has documented numerous cases where forgiveness is inappropriately seen as a therapeutic goal because of the therapist's inability to cope with the client's anger. This is a serious problem for survivors seeking professional help, for in its

---

[2] Janet Pais, *Suffer the Children: A Theology of Liberation by a Victim of Child Abuse*, (Mahwah; Paulist Press, 1991), p.53.

own way it can reproduce elements of the original abuse, where their feelings were not respected or acknowledged. Counselors who cannot cope with the expression of anger can in their own way add to the abuse already suffered.

Suppressed anger will often surface in inappropriate ways, directed towards inappropriate objects and persons. It will form an undercurrent in relationships, unsettling consciousness but never objectified. The anger which emerges as the person moves to being a survivor, on the other hand, becomes more focused, since it begins to recognize its true object, its true cause. Such anger can be very intense but it is not inappropriate and it does not lash out in all directions.

## THE DESCENT INTO HELL

> To search for insight into one's relations with others is ... like a deliberate descent into hell.[3]

The movement out of the hell of private suffering is not a simple process. If anything it involves a deeper descent into hell. The poet Dante knew this when he wrote his *Divine Comedy*. With his guide, Virgil, he discovers that there is a way out of hell, but it is not found by climbing up to the outer circles, where there is less suffering. Rather it is found by moving down into the deepest pit, into the very presence of Satan himself.

Janet Pais describes this process so eloquently that we cannot hope to improve upon her account. She writes:

> The inner healing process of relationship with the child-self consists of series of descents into the horrors of the past. The discoveries become successively more devastating, but each descent, if the true significance of feelings and memories is understood, brings greater inner strength and the ability to withstand something worse the next time. Some of the same discoveries are made over and over, but each time in a new way, in greater depth and with greater clarity. Prayer is a constant source of strength and hope.
>
> Eventually this process leads to the reawakening of feelings such as humiliation and shame, the awareness of weaknesses and

---

[3] Dunne, p.43, cf. Doran, p.243.

needs, and finally reactivation of intense self-hatred on a conscious level. An inner voice attacks every imperfection, every weakness, every need. The abuse victim feels unworthy of love and would rather be dead. The early crisis is re-engaged, and for healing to occur a new solution must be found. But the old solution continues to present itself as the only way out: "I must reject this weakness, this imperfection, this shame, this need. I must perfect myself and then I will be lovable."[4]

To experience this attack of the inner voice is to experience the very voice of the Satan, the Accuser.[5] It is to be in the deepest pit of hell, and the greatest temptation and the greatest danger is suicide.[6] Yet there is a way out through this inner torment. Perseverance, trust in God's grace, friends that one can turn to in times of need; most helpful of all is a guide who has been there before and knows there is a way out. All these can help to lead one out of the hell of the night of private suffering into the light of day. Alice Miller continually stresses the need for an "enlightened witness" to help the abused person, as Virgil helped Dante.[7]

One might even see that Jesus himself experienced such torment. The ancient Apostles' Creed spoke of Jesus' descent into hell. In its own way the tradition affirms that Jesus too knew of "the hell of the night of private suffering." He knew the accusations of the Satan, the attack on every limitation, weakness and need. His only solution, his only resort, was to abandon himself to the love of his Father, to commend his spirit to Him.

## THE NIGHT OF THE SUFFERING OF COMPASSION AND FORGIVENESS

Commenting on the work of John Dunne, Robert Doran writes:

> There is the hell of the night of private suffering, the suffering of isolation and victimization; and there is the night of the suffering

---

[4] Pais, p.96.

[5] Cf. N. Ormerod, *Grace and Disgrace*, pp.157–160.

[6] Cf. Ellen Bass and Laura Davis, *The Courage to Heal*, (Harper Perennial, 1988), pp.202–3.

[7] See for example Alice Miller's *Breaking Down the Wall of Silence*, (London; Virgo Press, 1992) and *Banished Knowledge: Facing Childhood Injuries*, (NY; Anchor Books, 1990).

of compassion and forgiveness. Between these two nights, as it were ... there lies the experience of the bliss of a day that supplants the first night and that cannot be supplanted by the second ... The hell of the night of private suffering is not redemptive. The night of the suffering of compassion and forgiveness is redemptive.[8]

If there is a message of hope for survivors it lies in the experience of the bliss that Dunne speaks of. Peace is possible, healing can occur, though it is neither automatic or to be taken for granted. Healing can be diverted into narcissistic self-absorption, into an anger which can never relent. However with time and patience healing can occur. Doran speaks of this healing as having "a rhythm that is far beyond the control" of human agencies.[9] Too often human agencies, particularly church authorities and some therapists, want to rush this process in order to find quick and easy solutions. There is no royal road to inner peace.

However the "bliss of the day" is not an end in itself. It leads into another night of suffering, the suffering of compassion and forgiveness. The question which is often placed before survivors, which they often ask themselves, is: "Will you ever be able to forgive?" What is important here is that forgiveness is not a precondition for healing, but may be its fruit. To attempt to forgive without being healed is to open oneself up to further victimization—"to submit to such victimization without oneself having been healed ... is masochism."[10]

How does one know whether one has been healed? Again Doran notes:

Perhaps one knows oneself to be healed only when precisely the same material dynamics of victimization that once drove one into the hell of private suffering now can be responded to with compassion and forgiveness.[11]

Ironically it is often the response of church authorities to disclosures of abuse which does recreate "precisely the same material

---

[8] Doran, p.114.
[9] Ibid., p.244.
[10] Ibid.
[11] Ibid., p.245.

dynamics of victimization" as the original abuse. Precisely where church authorities should be assisting in a work of grace, they are revictimizing the survivor. As Jesus said to Nicodemus, "You a teacher in Israel and you do not know these things!" (John 3:10).

Yet what does forgiveness mean? What does it mean when we say "I forgive you" to someone who has violated trust, body and soul? How can it be more than a denial of the suffering of the survivor?

## THE PLACE OF FORGIVENESS—NOT EXCUSING

It can be easy to excuse someone their sins of sexual abuse—he didn't know what he was doing, he was under pressure, he was not attending to his own needs, he was over-working, he was just doing what a man does. Often when we do this we can even think of ourselves as being good Christians—we must forgive one another, not seven times, but seventy-seven times, just as Jesus taught us (cf. Matthew 18:21). Yet to make excuses for abusers is not the same as to forgive them. Often to excuse them is to allow them to continue an abusive relationship which keeps the victim a victim, with no conversion in the abuser.

Excuses minimize the damage which has been done to the abused person, dismissing their suffering by making it less important than the suffering which will occur within the abuser if he is confronted with the full reality of his actions. Asking survivors to excuse or minimize the damage which has been done to them is saying to them again that their suffering is not important, that they are not important. Survivors are explicitly told, "I feel so sorry for the man, poor man!"; "what about his career?"; "but he's a good minister"; or "I can sympathize with both sides." The latter sounds eminently reasonable, but is in fact inappropriate if the injustice is not being adequately confronted.

Women in particular suffer from the problem of confusing excusing the abuser with forgiving them. Women are socialized to consider their own suffering as less significant than the suffering of significant males—fathers, brothers, husbands, sons, ministers. Their own needs must be repressed, ignored because they have learnt from childhood that being female means being a second class citizen or, worse still, being a non-person. When this is coupled with the Christian message of forgiveness and submission, the repression of women's needs is turned into a religious virtue. Being a victim can even give one a sense of religious self-righteousness. Indeed feminist theologians have often pointed out that the notion that "pride is the root of all sin" is a very male notion. In women the "root of sin" is more a failure of self-assertion, an undue submission which reflects a damaged sense of their own dignity.

For a woman to break out from being a victim and become a survivor, then, means fighting not only her socialization but also her religious feelings. It feels so wrong to confront the perpetrator with what they have done, to demand justice from authorities, to seek to have her own hurt and injury acknowledged and healed. It means going against everything she has learned from childhood. It takes courage and determination, and most of all God's grace, but the alternative is often to slip back into being a victim.

So forgiveness is not just about excusing, denying or minimizing the action of the abusive person. True forgiveness means placing before the sinner the full reality of what they have done, and in the face of this full reality offering forgiveness. This is one of the lessons of the death and resurrection of Jesus. In the passion of Jesus God reveals to us the full reality, the full ugliness, of human sinfulness. In the crucifixion of Jesus we see our willingness to sacrifice an innocent person in order to maintain a sinful status quo. It is only in knowing this reality that we can speak of the divine forgiveness. Anything less than this does not take sin as seriously as it needs to be taken. Anything less is a denial of the dignity of the victim.

Just as the process of healing cannot be controlled, so too no-one can force a person to forgive her abuser. Forgiveness can be the fruit of the healing process. It is an act of self-transcendence, a going beyond the self that one is, to a new, fuller self. It does involve a suffering, an offered suffering, not the suffering of abuse, of victimization, but a suffering of compassion. It cannot be demanded or expected, but must be a free gift, otherwise it just furthers the process of victimization.

In the seeking of forgiveness by the abusive person it is important that they actually know what it is they have done. Offers of apologies from perpetrators are often not only minimal but also meaningless since they do not even know what it is they are apologizing for. It is one of the paradoxes of abusive people that they can simultaneously beg for forgiveness and deny or minimize the wrong they have done. Again this can play on the religious beliefs of the survivor to rush into a premature forgiveness. Until the abuser comes to sufficient self-knowledge, through therapy and other personal support, for example, his apology is meaningless, and often it will only be through the continued confrontation by a good therapist or the survivor that there will be the necessary pressure for self-knowledge to occur.

## RESPONSES OF CHURCH AUTHORITIES

For church officials who may be called in to oversee such a process it will look as if it is the survivor who is now on the attack and the abuser who is being victimized. They may see the abuser, with whom they will often unconsciously identify, as having suffered enough and they may begin to feel sorry for him. Abusers are, of course, quite capable of playing on such sympathies for their own short-term benefit.

As a consequence, church officials will often put extreme pressure on victims to forgive and forget, to put the past behind them and get on with their lives.

> One survivor, looking for recognition of the seriousness of the harm done to her was referred by a responsible church authority to Jesus' words, "Let he who has not sinned cast the first stone." Hers were not stones cast by a number of privileged men at a defenceless woman with death as a possible consequence! It was a calling of a privileged person to account by a relatively powerless, wounded one. The stark differences were obviously not recognized.

All this will occur before the perpetrator has made an adequate apology. Further, church officials seem to place the greater burden of the process upon the survivor for they do not match pressure to forgive with a commensurate pressure on the perpetrator to make amends or offer restitution, which is also part of the Christian

43

tradition of repentance. For example, the tax collector Zaccheus offered to make good all that he had stolen plus more as a part of his repentance.

Such actions by church officials short-circuit the whole process of healing, both for the survivor and the abuser. Those who are called upon to help abusers come to grips with their actions need to journey with them, not cut the journey short. They need to exercise a "tough love." Respect for the dignity of the survivor demands that no minimization should occur. Only a full acknowledgment based on a clear understanding of what they have done, plus some offer of restitution for what the abuse has robbed from the survivor, constitutes a real apology.

Church authorities typically use other means also to avoid the demands of real healing. They offer the kind of sympathy which does not acknowledge the survivor's dignity or need to be heard. Survivors will be patronized, offered "prayers for their healing" as though the issue is one of the survivor's emotional disturbance and not one of justice. They will be offered sympathy for "the justice they don't see themselves" as receiving. Church officials can underestimate the costliness of real healing by responding primarily in financial terms. Settling out of court or payment for therapy expenses are only part of what is needed.

Worse still, the need for healing can be discounted altogether by church authorities who do not believe the survivor's account or who blame them in some way. It may be suggested to an adult survivor of childhood sexual abuse that they are fabricating memories. Survivors of adult abuse may be thought to be lying. They find themselves cross-examined as though it is they who are on trial. Or they are accused of wanting retribution, of wanting only compensation, attacking the church or of being mutually responsible—"You were an adult after all," or "You were asking for it."

In all, rather than assisting the process of healing, church officials deliver what amounts to a second round of abuse, only adding insult to injury. They drive survivors to explore legal options that in many cases they would not have considered.

We will continue our discussion of these and other aspects of the responses of church authorities in Chapter Five.

AFFIRMATION OF FAITH

I believe in one God, the Mother,
giver of birth and rebirth
creator of the unseen world
within the world we see.

I believe in Jesus Christ
the only true Saviour
who suffered, was victim
and was raised

I believe that to forgive sin
does not mean excusing it.
That to grow I must embrace the victim child within,
that tears are a solution,
that anger restores strength and stature
and to pray is no easy way through.

I believe the Kingdom has not yet come,
that there are oppressors and oppressed,
the oppressed feel blame, oppressors claim to be blameless,
there is much to be reversed.

That the Kingdom will only come
when we feel for the hurt of victims
the horror of all exploitation,
let rage empower action.

# GOING PUBLIC—LAZARUS EMERGES FROM THE TOMB

The suffering of the victim is the "hell of the night of private suffering." It occurs in secret, in the privacy of depression and shame, afraid to show its face to the public for fear of increasing the already overpowering burdens of guilt. It is like an insidious cancer eating away at the soul. As the abused person moves from being a victim to being a survivor, however, her suffering will cease to be a private matter, an inner shame, and may become more and more public. At first it may be spoken of to a small circle of friends and family. It may involve informing relevant church authorities of the activities of the abuser. In frustration and outrage at the church's responses, it may involve speaking to the media or seeking redress from the judicial system.

There is a power to public suffering which is prophetic in nature. The prophets often grieved publicly at Israel's failure to uphold the Covenant with Yahweh. According to Walter Brueggemann this public grief had the power to break through the numbness, the deadened awareness, that comes with accommodation to a sinful status quo.[12] Breaking the silence means that survivors hear each other also and take courage from the fact that they are not alone, that others have broken out of numbness and shame. This can be an important healing moment for survivors.

In the churches at present we have accommodated ourselves to a sinful status quo, in which we are willing to tolerate the sexual acting out of ministers, so long as it is kept secret so that there is no public scandal. The public suffering of survivors makes a lie of the silent hope that such activity "isn't really harmful." It threatens to break through the denial and minimization not only of the abuser, but of those who implicitly tolerate and hence collude with his abusive activities.

It is not surprising then that just like the prophets, survivors who "go public" are not welcome figures. Yet often they feel forced to do so simply because of the denial and minimization they experience from church authorities. They are reluctant prophets. Like Jeremiah they will say:

I do not know how to speak: I am a child. (Jer 1:6)

Abused persons often feel like children who are speaking out, looking to the church and demanding a parent's protective love. Yet such a demand is an accusation of the failure to provide that protection in the past. It is a prophetic word that the churches often do not want to hear.

To the abused person the experience of moving from victimhood to being a survivor can feel like being raised from the dead. Their years as a victim are the dead years, the years in the tomb, years of inner pain and decay. The catalytic actions which precipitate their movement out of this state become powerful signs of God's personal presence in their life, a grace which takes them

---

[12] W. Brueggemann, *The Prophetic Imagination*, (Philadelphia; Fortress Press, 1978) p.58ff.

from death to life, freeing them from the bonds of guilt and shame. For them it is as if they are Lazarus come out of the grave:

> Jesus cried out in a loud voice, 'Lazarus, come out!' The dead man came out, his feet and hands bound with strips of material, and a cloth over his face. Jesus said to them "Unbind him, let him go free." (John 11:43–44)

Nothing can be such a sure sign of the presence of God's activity as raising from the tomb a soul which has inwardly died.

Yet significantly, immediately following the raising of Lazarus, John's gospel portrays the chief priests and Pharisees as plotting to kill Jesus. Those who should have been most attuned to the presence and activity of God are those who are most threatened. The raising of Lazarus threatens to break through all our preconceptions of where God is and what God can do. Accordingly the chief priests and Pharisees decided not only to kill Jesus but, to remove the evidence of God's activity, also to kill Lazarus:

> Then the chief priests decided to kill Lazarus as well, since it was on his account that many of the Jews were leaving them and believing in Jesus. (John 12:10–11)

Church officials who find themselves denying the claims of survivors, of minimizing the activities of, or even protecting, abusers, of denying or delaying justice, can find themselves in the position of these same high priests, of trying to push Lazarus back into the tomb! Rather than rejoicing with the survivors at their new life, with the activity of God in their life, they would rather see them dead.

> Mary was a survivor of severe childhood sexual abuse by a priest. The abuse went on for five years. She had been painfully coming to grips with the abuse in therapy and finally developed the courage to disclose what had happened to the appropriate church official. During the interview he asked her what would be gained by pursuing this matter. After all, if these things happened, they happened thirty years or more ago; the alleged molester may well have stopped behaving in this way; and he may even have repented.
>
> Mary looked around the room, not quite knowing what to say. She noticed a crucifix on the coffee table and she recalled the events of Easter—that time of year had just passed. In a moment of

inspiration, Mary picked up the crucifix, held it up in the air and stated, "We remember this at every Eucharist and every Easter, but this happened 2000 years ago!"

## WHO IS GOD, WHERE DOES GOD STAND?

The ultimate questions that Christian survivors of abuse by church ministers must ask are, "Who is God? Where does God stand?" This is particularly significant, since to be abused by someone in ministry is to feel as if one is being abused by God. The minister carries a religious authority, so that his abusive actions throw the victim's image of God into total disarray. Even God cannot be trusted.

At some time or other most of us have a fearful image of God. We see God as an angry judge, a God who is just waiting for us to make a mistake in order to punish us, possibly with eternal suffering in hell. Most of us pick this up as children at some time, and sadly many carry this image into adult life. For such people religion is full of fear, a process of placating God's anger and trying to get on with life. For this God sexuality is a dark and evil force, full of sin and shame. It makes no distinction between victims and perpetrators, since both are touched by the evil of sex.

Such an image of God has nothing to do with the truth of God. Such a God is more to do with the accusing voice of the Satan, the twisted super-ego, forever putting us down, demanding ever greater sacrifices to keep it happy. Yet it is one of the consequences of any type of abuse that such an image of God becomes deeply internalized, deeply embedded in the heart and soul of the victim. Where the abuser is a church minister the message can become, "This abuse is God's punishment for your sins."

For the survivor moving out of victimhood, part of the process involves a necessary revision of her image of God, a rejection of the God of punishment, of unreal guilt, of hell-fire for the smallest transgression. But what is there to replace it with, what can do justice to her new experience?

It is commonly said that "we have replaced the old God of fear with the God of love. We don't preach hell-fire any more, just love and peace." "Feel bad" religion has been replaced by "feel good" religion. This is the God of unconditional love, a God who does not even require real repentance and conversion. For this God sexuality is natural and good. It makes no distinction between victims and perpetrators because there are no victims and there are no perpetrators. There is no sexual exploitation, since sex is good and natural and we all have equal power to exercise our freedom in this regard.

Yet the survivor does not "feel good" at all. She is struggling with guilt, shame and anger. She may be rejecting of the old God of guilt but she can find no home with the "feel good" God either. Too often the God of love and peace is really the God of a romantic illusion, an illusion which speaks of love and forgiveness as if they are simple and without cost. Indeed ministers of "feel good" religion can be as abusive and exploitative as "feel bad" ministers, because they are just as out of touch with the pain and struggle of people's lives. The "feel good" God is not adequate to the experience of survivors and in its own way this attitude furthers their marginalization in the church.

To discover the truth about God, to know who God is and where God stands, we need only look at the life and death of Jesus. Clearly Jesus is not about a "feel bad" God who is just waiting for us to put a foot wrong. He does teach us about a loving God, who cares about us intimately—"every hair on your head has been counted." Yet just as equally he is not about a "feel good" God, where nothing really matters and no-one gets hurt. Jesus feels for the victims of injustice and denounces those who oppress them. He gets angry and calls those who exploit and abuse to judgment. Indeed he identifies with victims, the poor, the outcast, the lepers, the public sinners, those who are victimized and abused by the religiously self-righteous, the priests, scribes and Pharisees. In his crucifixion this identification becomes complete, he becomes the Victim, who has voluntarily taken on the suffering of abuse, so that in the resurrection he may show us the fullness of being a Survivor. The God that Jesus reveals stands with victims and with survivors and against those who abuse their power, in whatever way they abuse.

For the God of Jesus, human sexuality is an area of brokenness and vulnerability, of power, exploitation and manipulation, as well as fruitfulness and love. Those who are broken and vulnerable need to be protected, to be in a safe environment where they can enter into the long and painful process of healing, so that they can experience the fullness of what human sexuality is meant to be. Those who manipulate and exploit are called to repent and change their ways. They must learn to identify with their victims and rediscover their own vulnerability and so enter themselves into the long and difficult process of healing. The God of Jesus stands with the victims of sexual abuse and against those who abuse, calling them to repent and make reparation for their misdeeds.

Does Jesus present a God of ultimate judgment? Undoubtedly yes. When Jesus speaks of judgment he often speaks of himself in terms of the enigmatic figure of "the Son of Man." Drawn from the Book of Daniel, this figure represents the whole people, Israel, who were suffering terrible religious persecution at the hands of Greek invaders. By presenting the Son of Man as a judgment figure, the author of Daniel is saying that human history will be judged, but it will be judged by its victims. When Jesus adopts this title for himself he maintains this significance. He will judge history, but he will do so by identifying with history's victims: "Whenever you did this to the least, you did it to me—whenever you failed to do so, you failed to do it to me" (cf. Mt 25:31ff).

### WHO IS GOD?

This was not God, the one I was taught,
distant Judge, Father, King, earth his dominion,
benign as long as ... loved you if ...
you follow the rules perfectly,
if you don't cry or be angry.
Obey or be out of grace,
in need of confession's magic.
This God needed Jesus sacrificed to be appeased,
not God, but a monster.

With it came a mute Madonna,
pale lifeless virgin
and sexuality that was shameful,
all up to the girl to keep herself unsullied,
to live in fear of sex and hell.

God of virgins and martyrs,
bringer of guilt and shame and death,
I reject you.

Then there was the God of romantic illusion,
of words that sound good,
love and life are simple, in the head,
avoids the Cross or mythologizes it.
Seductive God of being good
is being nice is feeling good, feeling free,
in truth, merely flight from earth.
Women on a pedestal, secretly despised.
God of lies,
I reject you too.

You God of all is well,
in truth, not a well
but a pit in which to fall
so evil has its way.

Thus I fell
when a guru stood before God
before me,
haloed in light,
came onto me
until I was lost in darkness.

It was God who found me
through friends surrounded me
with Her warm waters of love
and breathed life into me.

She is the God of Life,
of laughter, equanimity,
sexual love given freely,
of tears and anger, outrage.

She is the God of Truth,
a light that casts all into stark relief.
With her comes the living Maria
who crushes serpents underfoot
and speaks out
against the God of guilt and death
and the God of lies.

I believe in the God who found me
in the mess of complex humanity
this God of feeling with,
of life rooted in the dirt of the earth,
for whom being good is being on the way.

The God I believe in redeems,
came to sacrifice Godself
to bring us peace.

In the next chapter we shall consider the situation of the abusive minister. It is perhaps a sobering thought for all abusers, whether sexual, psychological, physical or whatever, that they will be judged by their victims. As Jesus warns his followers:

Anyone who is an obstacle to bring down one of these little ones who have faith in me would be better drowned in the depths of the sea with a great millstone around his neck. (Matthew 18:6)

CHAPTER FOUR

# THE ABUSIVE
# MINISTER

I
t is time now to turn our attention to the nature of the abusive minister. Here it is important that church authorities and the general public learn to identify sexually abusive ministers so that they can protect both the vulnerable and the churches from the damage they do. Early identification can prevent years of suffering and pain for all concerned.

One difficulty here is that abusive ministers are camouflaged by a culture which encourages those with power, most often men, to have a sense of entitlement more than to act responsibly.

In their ethical study of pastoral sexual abuse, *Sex in the Parish*, Lebacqz and Barton develop three categories of ministers who involve themselves sexually with those in their pastoral care. These are referred to as the normal neurotic, the wanderer and the offender.[1] We shall use these as convenient categories to distinguish different types of sexual misconduct among ministers.

"The normal neurotic minister" is one who falls in love with or is otherwise sexually attracted to some person in his pastoral care. A relationship develops during which the minister experiences the normal struggles of a developing loving, but difficult, relationship. During it all he maintains a sense of responsibility for the good of the other person and in the end he "does the right thing by her." In various situations this may involve breaking off the relationship (for the sake of his or her marriage) with offers of restitution for any harm done, or marrying her (which

---

[1] Lebacqz and Barton, p.129.

may mean, in the Catholic Church, leaving ministry altogether). Such a minister will experience the situation as painful and perhaps destructive of himself and the woman involved but will seek to act in a morally responsible fashion.

"The wanderer" on the other hand will "fall" in and out of love with any number of women in his pastoral care. He is a very needy person who is vaguely aware of his needs and hopes that one or other of his relationships might finally meet his needs for love and assurance. His main problem is emotional immaturity. He has a vague sense that what he is doing is not adequate, but this only feeds his insecurity and may lead to further acting out. His behavior might be described as "addictive," a love or sex addict as he wanders from one failed relationship to another.

Finally there is "the offender." Such ministers have no real sense that their actions are wrong; indeed they may feel a sense of being entitled to their actions. They are predators of vulnerable women with no conscience about their actions. They are manipulative, emotionally coercive and controlling. They will have a series of rationalizations which justify their abusive actions, from blaming the victims to describing themselves as channels of cosmic energy. Marie Fortune describes them as sociopaths. To outward appearances they may be attractive, even charismatic, yet this facade hides a sinister interior which is extremely damaging to their victims.

Now these categories are not fixed for any particular minister. Ministers who begin as normal neurotics may move down the scale, given the right psychological predisposition and a gradual hardening of their hearts to their own and others' suffering. Such a moral decline can occur if appropriate action is not taken in identifying and remedying sexually abusive actions at the start.

We would now like to explore further the situation of the offender category. This is by far the most damaging, if not the most common. It is also the most deceptive since to outside appearances, such ministers often appear as capable, even exemplary in their calling.

## NARCISSISM AND THE ARCHETYPAL OFFENDER[2]

In an article, aptly named "Soul Stealing: Power Relations in Pastoral Sexual Abuse," Pamela Cooper-White describes the "typical" pastoral sexual abuser in the following terms:

> The internal dynamics at work in these men may include: history of an abusive childhood; low self-esteem and a fear of failure; deeply held traditional values about male and female roles, however disguised in liberal rhetoric; poor impulse control; a sense of entitlement, of being above the law, or other narcissistic traits; difficulty accepting responsibility for mistakes and difficulty establishing appropriate intimate relationships and friendships with male peers (he may have what Mary Pellauer calls a "Lone Ranger" style of ministry).[3]

In what follows we would like to present an analysis of the narcissistic personality and how it fits into the picture of the offender in pastoral sexual abuse. This analysis attempts to address what is a common problem in dealing with offenders, that is that they are outwardly very attractive, even charismatic personalities. This makes it very difficult for people to see them for the dangerous people they are. The analysis below is archetypal. No offender may match exactly the description given, though they may correspond to several of the key features.

> I thought I had a wonderful brother in Christ. We discussed theology together and through this my minister encouraged me to grow. He also liked to talk over parish matters with me. I saw him as a gentleman who treated me with great respect. He was the first person ever in my life to say I was beautiful.
>
> Then I found it was all seduction.
>
> We were having a wonderful prayer session together. I was communing with God, quite oblivious to the minister personally, when he asked me to masturbate him. I was so shocked I became incapable of moving, as though I was in his grip physically. He left the room.

---

[2] In his book *The Abuse of Power* (Nashville; Abingdon Press, 1991), James Newton Poling presents a similar analysis of what he calls the "grandiose self," cf. pp.67 ff.

[3] Cf. *The Christian Century*, 20 Feb 1991, pp.196 ff.

After that incident I tried to protect myself as best I could, but eventually he sexually assaulted me.

It was the ultimate betrayal. Someone who would use God to get sex. He got spirituality and sexuality mixed up. He got God and himself mixed up. He thought he could do no wrong. I concluded that he was not about God at all, but about power. He was actually a wolf in sheep's clothing.

The worst part of it all was losing my friends and community. The minister was afraid I'd tell people, so he turned them against me by telling lies about me. It became impossible for me to stay.

## THE VOICE OF THE SATAN

In his previous book, *Grace and Disgrace*, Neil Ormerod, co-author of the present book, presents an analysis of the voice of the Satan, the Accuser, who harries us with a constant stream of accusations, undermining our self-esteem, leading to self-doubt and a primal sense of guilt which we call original sin. This inner voice of accusation drives us onwards, never to be satisfied with the good we achieve, always demanding more than we can give, always seeking new sacrifices to appease the anger within.[4]

Without denying the experience described in *Grace and Disgrace*, we have come to realize that this picture is incomplete in terms of the inner actions of the Accuser. In the above account there always remains a critical distance between the voice of the Accuser and the ego of the person experiencing these accusations. It becomes an experience of being accused, of being put down, of self-esteem being constantly undermined. Psychologically such a condition can be identified with perfectionistic and self-destructive tendencies. Yet this is not the only possibility and an alternative can occur which is far more dangerous and destructive.

In cases of more severe psychological damage than that which is described above, the internalized voice of the Accuser can become so strong, so insistent, that the person experiencing it can no longer endure it. Since they cannot get rid of it of themselves, the alternative is to identify with it. The critical distance between the ego and the Accuser begins to vanish and they take on the

---

[4] Cf. *Grace and Disgrace*, esp. pp.157 ff.

voice of the Accuser themselves. In psychological terms this corresponds to a narcissistic neurotic tendency.[5] Significantly, best-selling author Scott Peck develops the category of "evil person" as a sub-category of the narcissistic personality and draws on the religious mythology of possession to explore it.[6]

When this happens the person no longer experiences him/herself as under the accusations of the Satan. They can achieve a state in which there is no longer any self-accusation, no longer any sense of self-criticism. Everything they do they do out of the highest possible motivations. All their intentions are pure and righteous. They are guided by the highest possible ideals. Whenever anyone questions their actions or intentions they reject them out of hand, accusing them of lies and calumnies, of malicious slander, or they turn it back onto the complainant with "What's your problem?" They will invoke the Gospel that we should not judge others and so no-one has the right to question or judge them. Yet such people become walking accusations of everyone else. Nothing is wrong with them, but everything is wrong with everyone else. Scott Peck speaks of such people as characterized by "their *absolute* refusal to tolerate the sense of their own sinfulness".[7]

However when the challenge to their virtue and intentions is strong enough or carries some recognized authority (if they still recognize another's authority!), the critical distance between the ego and the Accuser is momentarily restored and the person begins to get in touch once again with the original pain of their life. They experience the full weight of the voice of the Accuser as leveled against them, leading to panic and despair. The contrast between the self-righteousness they project and the accusations they are confronted with is so strong that they fall apart.

## COVERT AND OVERT IDENTIFICATION WITH THE VOICE

Identification with the voice of the Accuser can come about in two ways, which may be labeled overt and covert.

---

[5] Narcissism is to be distinguished from mere egotism. Egotism arises from an unwillingness to consider the other, narcissism from an inability, cf Doran, p.235.
[6] Cf. *People of the Lie*, (London; Rider, 1988), p.77ff, p.182ff.
[7] Ibid, p.71.

Overt identification with the voice of the Accuser is seen in the abusive, aggressive person who has derogatory opinions about everyone and everything and lets everyone know as often as possible. Such people are not attractive, indeed they are generally repulsive, opinionated and quite pathetic. While they make life hell for themselves and anyone near to them there is no difficulty in identifying them or the brokenness they carry in their heart. Unloved and brutalized as children, they can find no other protection from their inner pain than to project it onto anyone who passes, which further increases their isolation and sense of rejection.

When such people attain some power over others, as parents or in their work, they invariably abuse their power, either psychologically, physically or sexually. However there is no confusing their abuse for anything other than what it is. Despite their claims to blamelessness, their abusive nature is obvious to everyone.

However there is a far more subtle form of identification that can take place, leading to far more subtle forms of abuse. It is more dangerous, particularly in religious settings. It is possible for there to be a covert identification with the voice of the Accuser. Such people do not become the loud-mouthed opinionated brutes who attack everything that moves. Rather they can be quite serene and peaceful, even highly attractive. They do not spend their energies in attacking others, rather they employ their talents in projecting an image of perfection and inner strength. These are the people who, everyone thinks, "have their act together." They do not need to force their opinions onto others, people seek out their opinion—though they will often collect around them types who will stroke their egos.

Such people do not have to put other people down, their mere presence is an accusation: "I have my act together, why don't you? If you were more like me you would be better off." Rather than see evil everywhere except in themselves, as in an overt identification, such people may not see evil anywhere: "Everything is beautiful. If you can't see it that way, all you need to do is to broaden your vision."

## THE RELIGIOUS GURU FIGURE AS ABUSER

Far from being seen as broken, such people appear healthy, religious and even holy. In a religious setting they may see themselves as living examples of God's graciousness. They may be attracted to ministry, and conversely, ministry may help reinforce their tendencies.[8] Indeed if one looks at the training methods for ministry within, for example, the Catholic Church up to the 1960s, the harrowing stories of physical deprivation, of psychological, physical and spiritual abuse, one would see them as reinforcing narcissism. Catholic seminaries and training colleges often had an explicit ethos of "breaking the person's spirit." To survive such a system required active suppression of one's pain, a splitting off from one's vulnerability, simply in order to survive. In some ways these institutes were breeding grounds for abusive personalities.

Such people may become religious gurus, teachers and preachers of high reputation and gather around themselves followers and disciples. This situation can lead to massive ego-inflation and they see themselves as above the law, beyond good and evil, living in a different realm from the rest of humanity—"I'm not like other people, I'm different. I don't have needs, or limits." The ego-inflation can become so great that they see themselves as a new incarnation of Christ, the return of the Messiah. Tragic examples are evident in such figures as David Koresh.

Yet as St Paul states, "Even Satan disguises himself as an angel of light" (2 Corinthians 11:14). All may not be what it seems. What seems like detachment may simply be dissociation from deeply repressed feelings. What seems like spontaneity may simply be reckless indifference. What seems like holy simplicity may simply be an irresponsible denial of the complexities of relationships and situations. The very qualities which make such people so attractive have what may be termed a mirror image where what had appeared as good and holy is inverted to become the opposite.

---

[8] The way in which ministry operates can in fact shield the minister from the forces which could break open such narcissism. Note also that Scott Peck, in *People of the Lie* claims that "evil people" often seek out the respectability of religion, cf. p.76. What could be more respectable than being a minister?

Eventually things begin to unravel for such people. Their narcissistic ego-inflation causes a loss of connection with reality. They begin to make mistakes. Their disconnectedness with their own limits pushes them to physical and mental exhaustion and eventual breakdown. Deeply repressed feelings will demand attention often at the cost of psychosis. Recklessness takes its toll in overwork, substance abuse and inattention to personal needs. An irresponsible denial of the complexity of relationships and situations leads to inevitable damage done to those around them, often in the form of sexual abuse.

It is in this time of unravelling that the person's tendency to deny and rationalize will come to the fore. One of the most striking features of perpetrators of sexual abuse is their ability to lie point-blank about their activities, to minimize their extent and to attempt to rationalize them as something other than they were; for instance, "I was just showing affection." Any handling of perpetrators which does not take this tendency seriously is just wasting the time of all involved.

## THE INITIAL DYNAMIC OF ABUSE

Invariably there will be those in the circle of followers who experience their own brokenness in terms of the persistent inner voice of the Accuser. To them the religious guru figure offers a picture of spiritual and psychological health. They are drawn into his circle looking for healing and spiritual guidance. They come in vulnerability and pain. Yet they find no healing, rather a silent accusation of their own brokenness.

Within the narcissistic guru-figure, however, the presence of a vulnerable person re-awakens patterns of his own vulnerability which was exploited in his own history of being abused. The vulnerability of the disciple becomes an invitation to exploitation, releasing a repetition compulsion of abuse, often in the form of sexual exploitation. Powerless as a previous victim of abuse, he is now able to exercise power over someone else and give vent to his narcissistic rage. However, given their psychological disposition, the disciples are likely to blame themselves for whatever happens in the relationship. Indeed they may see themselves as leading their guru astray, leading him into sin, even destroying his ministry. They will try to keep their activities with the guru secret, partly out of shame and a sense of guilt, partly out of a felt need to protect the guru. After all, in their eyes he can do no wrong. His ministry needs to be protected "for the greater good." They become the sacrifice he demands, indeed he even feeds off their vulnerability to further inflate his ego.

This leads to a stark disparity between the public persona and certain private relationships of the guru. The public appearance may be one of warmth, wisdom, grace and wholeness. The private experience of those whom he ensnares into abusive relationships is one of callous indifference, hard-heartedness and a disconnectedness with his own inner world and needs. In public the guru can speak passionately about the highest of ideals. In private he can be destroying those same ideals in the hearts of those he has ensnared.

Rather than finding the healing they had hoped for, these victims suffer a further blow to their damaged self-esteem, leading to suicidal thoughts, loss of faith, generalized anxiety and despair. Indeed because the abuse comes from a person identified as God's medium or representative, it seems as if the divine Himself is rejecting and abusing them.

### PRINCE OF DARKNESS

Children of light,
the prince of darkness stalks about
clothed in white.

He appears as a prince
with a winning welcome, charm and eloquence—
it leaves you prey to acquiescence.

He begins by inquiring about your needs
and ends by informing you.
He walks with you awhile on your way,
long enough to elicit your faith in him,
then seduces you down
a different, darker direction.

He offers a feast—it's mouth-watering illusion.
When you begin to eat
you're left hungry and in confusion.

The prince's beauty is an empty shell,
his insides full of corrosion,
he seeks to fill his unfeeling void
by feeding from your life-blood.

Know the prince of darkness
prefers places of power.
Look out for him standing around the altar
or poised in the seat of judgment.
Seek no kudos
from being close to such charisma
for fear you are enlisted only as its servant,
for tyranny can appear as regency
and always cloaks itself in secrecy.

## REFLECTIONS ON THE NATURE OF EVIL

One of the major difficulties people have in identifying such actions as evil is that the private actions are so at odds with the public face of the abuser. And it is true that the actions of the abuser do not necessarily flow from some form of deliberate decision to harm anyone. Because he does not intend to harm anyone, some think that his actions cannot be that wrong or evil. Yet this is to misunderstand the nature of evil.

Evil rarely arises from a deliberate decision to do what one knows clearly to be harmful. This would simply be sadism. More often it results from series of small decisions which shape one's character into greater and greater distortions so that one simply no longer knows right from wrong. This is the danger of the "normal neurotic" who fails to act in a morally responsible manner and slips into ever greater abusive relationships. Under such circumstances the evil that is eventually chosen actually appears as a good. The patterns of rationalization become so deeply rooted that in fact vices can be interpreted as virtues. Chronic overwork is said to be "religious commitment"; sexual abuse is said to be "showing affection"; a lack of critical self-awareness is said to be "other centredness."

In such cases the nature of evil is not seen simply in the deliberate decisions of the abuser but in the compulsiveness of his actions. There is no intention to harm anyone, but in fact real harm is done. The problem is not intention, but inattention, inattention to the suffering he inflicts. The outcome is that very real and significant harm can be done by persons who would never think of themselves as ever harming anyone. Yet often they could not do more harm if they had been deliberate about their actions. Indeed it is often the thoughtlessness of the actions which identify them as abusive and hence evil.[9]

## REPEATING THE CYCLE OF ABUSE

For those who manage to extricate themselves from such abusive relationships, it is almost impossible to bring to light exactly what has happened to them. The public persona of the guru figure is so strong, projecting such wholeness and goodness, that other people will find it almost impossible to believe the stories of abuse. If survivors try to go public they can expect to be ignored, ridiculed and even blamed. "It never happened, and even if it did it must have been your fault." "He was as much your victim as you were his." Victims are portrayed as "throwing themselves at him." Yet this is simply not the case. They are truly the victims of abuse, and further ridicule and blame simply perpetuate the cycle of abuse they have already experienced. Again they are being sacrificed in order to maintain the public persona of the guru, which must be maintained at all cost. Far too many people have far too much invested in it to allow it to be destroyed by a few unfortunate victims.

The strongest defense will come from those closest to the guru figure. These will be the people who have tried to emulate the guru, to adopt his manner of living and value system. These are the ones who have most to lose, who have invested most in his public persona. They may even have been victims of his abuse, who have sought refuge from their pain in the narcissism exhibited by the guru. Such people have become acolytes to the evil which infects the guru, themselves radiating, or at least attempting to radiate, the same sense of "having it all together," of wholeness

---

[9] Of itself this could be used as an argument for a personified agent of evil. The abusers are not being deliberate in their abuse yet the pattern of their actions displays an intelligence which is clearly not their own. As noted above, such personalities give rise to the mythology of possession.

and grace, yet at the same time leaving those around them feeling inadequate and accused.

However for most, public exposure of the abusive activities of the guru leads to bewilderment, uncertainly, fear and indecision. In this sense the abuse which the guru has perpetrated becomes an abuse of the whole community. All have had their trust betrayed. Indeed in a Christian church community the whole church is betrayed, for ministers who act in such a fashion undermine the trust on which ministry operates. Worse still, their actions have perpetuated the sacrificial cycle of innocent victims which Jesus' death was meant to end. The early Christian community knew that the sacrifice of Jesus was "once and for all." No further sacrifices were needed, nor could they be tolerated. Christian ministers who sexually abuse those in their care pervert the heart of the Christian message. They become counter-signs of the Kingdom; rather than being alter-Christus, they become anti-Christus, for they have used the ministry of Christ to undo the work of Christ.

### EVIL'S WORST

Evil's worst
when wolves take on
the robes of God's word
and waste and woo away from.
Their waters are murky with death
but they speak of reflection,
and let the reflected light
put them centre-stage.

Evil's worst bore down on Jesus
but He would not be fashioned in their image
or cower in this carpentry.
Victim with a difference.

Nor did he condemn.
Even in death undeserved
He wouldn't play the game
and prayed for them.

No. Jesus is proclaimer
and kneels to wash our dirty feet.

Life fully pulsing in Him,
emptying, so we feel strong.
Light that sheds Himself on us.
And in the height of His persecution
we are lifted up.

## THE ARCHETYPAL OFFENDER AND THE VAMPIRE MYTH

There are many myths which attempt to capture the plight of the narcissistic ego-inflated person. There is of course the original myth of Narcissus, who fell in love with his own reflection. The story of Icarus, who flew too close to the sun, also captures the situation. Modern stories of Faust, who sold his soul to the devil for the sake of knowledge, and the figure of Don Juan, are examples of narcissistic ego-inflation with demonic overtones. Indeed the romantic idealism of the eighteenth and nineteenth centuries was attracted to such figures. They are not unattractive in themselves and often they seem to act out of the highest, even heroic, motivations. Yet their ego-inflation leads to a disconnectedness with reality and their eventual destruction.

Most of these myths deal with the progressive development of the narcissistic ego-inflated personality and their tragic end. However there is one myth which we would like to suggest is particularly appropriate for an analysis of the case of pastoral sexual abuse as perpetuated by the archetypal offender. The myth in question is the vampire myth.

The sexual-erotic overtones of the vampire myth are well known. Of their female victims, the vampires are portrayed as seducers. Yet the goal of the vampire is not sexual, but the drawing of blood. The ulterior motive of their actions is to feed off the life-blood of their victims, to restore their own life-force. Energized by their victims, they lead a life which externally is full of charm and sophistication. This, however, covers up the secrecy of their true identity.

Now we shall apply this to the case of the narcissistic ego-inflated minister engaged in pastoral sexual abuse. Such ministers may engage in sexual activity, yet not necessarily for its own sake. Indeed it is possible for them to suffer from some type of impotence, so that they may not even experience sexual arousal in quite erotic situations. Their interest then is not in itself sexual, but in the psychic energy which they can draw off their victims. In the vampire myths this is symbolized by the drawing of blood. The greater the sexual arousal, the more energy they can draw from their victims, so they will continue to push sexual boundaries, even though they themselves need not be aroused. Because of this some may not even see their activities as sexual at all. The victims may experience the highs of sexual arousal at the time, but afterwards feel themselves as empty, hollow, used and so fall into depression, self-blame, guilt and shame.

Such ministers will often bring energy and enthusiasm to their ministry. This was the case for example in the situation portrayed by Marie Fortune in *Is Nothing Sacred?*. The minister brought new life to a pedestrian parish, while conducting an horrific campaign of sexual abuse. Yet, mixing such energy and charisma with the sexual abuse is not a coincidental occurrence. It is rather the other side of the coin. The sexual activities are being used to energize the ministry in what could be seen as a Faustian bargain with the devil. The life drawn from their victims further inflates the abusive ministers' egos, leading to further dissociation from reality and the necessity of even further abuse to sustain their ministry.

There are a number of elements in the vampire myth which parallel the analysis we have made above.

1. Significant victims of the vampire become vampires themselves. Those "killed" by the vampire return as undead to seek out further victims. Above we noted that one escape for victims from the voice of the Accuser is for themselves to adopt the narcissism of the abuser. In doing so they become, like the abuser, dead inside, out of touch with their own inner life. Outwardly they appear to "have their act together," but this becomes simply denigration of those around them. They get trapped in the same evil which infects the abuser.

2. The vampire has no reflection in a mirror. The mirror symbolizes access to the inner life. In the mirror we see our true selves, not just the outward appearance. Yet here the mirror reveals nothing. The inner life of the narcissist is empty, all feelings dead. They cannot afford to see their true selves, for it would be in such stark contrast to the image of goodness which they project. In

symbolic terms this corresponds to the Scholastic doctrine that evil has no substance, that it does not really "exist," but is rather a lack of being.

3. The vampire is repulsed by the cross. The life of the sexual abuser, particularly in a Christian minister, is antithetical to the cross of Jesus. Where Jesus sacrifices his life in a love which overcomes evil, the abusive minister sacrifices his sexual victims to further inflate his ego and perpetuate the evil within him. The abuser cannot face the reality of the cross of Jesus, which is such a contradiction to his own life.

4. The vampire is destroyed by daylight. The vampire only operates by night. Similarly the abuser's activities must be kept secret, must be kept "in the dark," if they are to continue. For example the abuser in Marie Fortune's account had more than one "fiancée" at one time, none of whom knew about the others. Once exposed to the light of truth the whole image projected by the abuser begins to disintegrate. It becomes more and more difficult to maintain as more and more people discover the truth. This can lead to a catastrophic deflation of the ego from which they may never recover. As the Johannine Jesus says to Nicodemus:

> ... people loved darkness rather than light because their deeds were evil. For all who do evil hate the light and do not come to the light, so that their deeds may not be exposed. (John 3:19–20)

5. Classically the death of the vampire is brought about by a stake through the heart. No other physical attack is effective. This gruesome yet powerful image symbolizes the hardness of heart of the narcissistic person. They have hardened their hearts to their own pain and so can no longer feel the pain of their victims. The stake through the heart symbolizes the fact that the hearts of such abusers must themselves be broken open, perhaps even by emotional violence, to get them in touch once more with their own inner pain. Only then will they get in touch with the truth of their own lives, the reality of their actions, and the effects on their victims. While it appears destructive, and in fact is destructive of the ego-inflated image, it is also redemptive since it leads onto a path to healing.

## COOPER-WHITE'S CHECK LIST

It is not difficult to examine the list of characteristics given by Cooper-White in terms of the above analysis.

A "history of abusive childhood" is often a causal factor in narcissism since it leads to a very deep-seated sense of "low self-esteem." Abused children experience themselves as basically unlovable, of no worth. Narcissism develops as a protective shield to such feelings which may be deeply repressed.

Such persons may display "deeply held traditional values about male and female roles" because of a resentment towards their mother, who either abused them or failed to protect them from abuse from their father. Traditional male and female roles emphasize the weakness and vulnerability of women and their dependence on men, and the subordination of female needs to those of men, especially in the area of sexuality. Holding such values is one way of getting back at women, who symbolize the original mother. The overt claim of such values is to "place women on a pedestal" but it is really a way of denying their true humanity and treating them as objects.

People who are abused have "poor impulse control" because they have never learnt restraint as a child. Their abuse was the product of "poor impulse control" of parents (or others) acting out of their own repetition compulsions. When they themselves are placed in positions of power as ministers (or parents) they will act as they were taught as children, to repeat the cycle of abuse.

## WHAT THE FUTURE MAY HOLD

The actions of the abusive minister may of course never come to light, or they may only come to light years after the event. His victims may take twenty or thirty years to emerge out of victimhood to become survivors. It is possible that by that stage the abuser has long ago finished his abusive activities. He has become a respected senior member of the church community who suddenly has to face his past history as a sexual abuser. Outwardly his life has been a success while inwardly his life has been a hollow sham. Indeed his whole spiritual life has been built on falsehood, since he has never really repented his destructive activities. Now this is exposed for all to see. Perhaps this situation is best expressed by an excerpt from the poem "Little Gidding" by T.S. Eliot. In this poem Eliot speaks of the "gifts reserved for age," the decaying body, the growing sense of impotence, and finally the pain of recollection of the past:

> Of all that you have done, and been; the shame
> Of motives late revealed, and the awareness
> Of things ill done and done to others' harm
> Which once you took as exercise of virtue.

The abuser lives in the illusion of his own goodness. He looks back on his past convinced of the goodness of his own motives. Yet the disclosure of his sexual abusive activities brings all this into question and reveals the great harm his noble intentions have achieved. Eliot sees a solution to the resulting malaise: one must pass through the refining purgatorial fire, "like a dancer," with graceful acceptance of a rhythm beyond one's control.

## CONCLUSION

In this chapter we have attempted to paint, in terms as stark as possible, a portrait of abusive ministers, since it is our experience that church authorities consistently underestimate the nature of the evil that they are dealing with. While they acknowledge the supreme value of religion, they fail to see that the perversion of this great good, as occurs in sexual abuse by ministers, constitutes a correspondingly greater evil. Their own minimizations of the evil involved in sexual abuse reinforces those of the abuser and can effectively prevent any serious investigation of the perpetrator. Until church officials see the abuser for who he really is they will not be motivated to act responsibly.

# CHAPTER FIVE

# PERSPECTIVES ON CHURCH RESPONSE

Disclosures of sexual impropriety or abuse usually lead to a very mixed response from church leaders who have the responsibility to address the situation. In this chapter we would like to consider the ways in which such leaders could respond, how they are perceived by survivors as responding and some of the reasons for this response. This will hopefully lead to more constructive policies from the churches in the future. Finally we consider principles which may be used in developing such policies.

## A SCALE OF RESPONSE

Disclosures of sexual misconduct, abuse or assault elicit various responses which may be placed on an increasing scale of ethical understanding on the part of church leaders. As one moves up the scale one is forced to reflect more deeply on the nature of the problem and hence one is required to act in a more decisive, forceful manner. Sadly most church leaders never get beyond the first level, so that their responses are generally weak and indecisive.

### * A failure of sexual ethics

The first level of response is to see the activities of the minister in terms of a violation of sexual ethics. By acting out with children or with those in his pastoral care, the minister is violating a Christian understanding of sexuality, which includes the notion of monogamous, mutually consenting sexual relations and, in the case of Catholics, of celibacy in ministry. While once such activities constituted a serious moral fault, a more liberal sexual ethic now

71

operative in society means that such violations, at least with adults, are seen as a question of mutual consent, they are "affairs," and so authorities tend to minimize the event and to blame the adult victim. Even child victims are said by abusers to have enjoyed their abuse or to have led the abuser on in some way.

That a violation of Christian sexual ethics has occurred should not be ignored, nor should it be played down. The failure of ministers to uphold the sexual moral standards of the Christian tradition is a serious problem for the churches given the counter-cultural nature of the Christian message in this area. The church loses credibility in the area of sexual morality when its ministers act out. The public cry of hypocrisy is raised, and so brings the churches into disrepute. This is not a small matter, though it is often minimized by reference to our common sinful nature: "we are all sinners"—or by talk of: "media hype" or "vindictive victims."

Yet such a response is inadequate. As we have constantly argued in this book it ignores the power relationship which exists between the minister and those in his pastoral care. The minister has access, because of his professional role, to intimate aspects of a person's life. There is an antecedent trust needed for any ministry to be able to operate. When such issues are raised we begin to move onto the second level of a possible response from church leaders.

### * A failure of professional ethics

The next level of response sees the sexual activities of the minister as undermining the antecedent trust which is necessary for ministry to operate. Such actions are "unprofessional" in much the same way as such behavior would be unprofessional in a doctor, counselor or teacher. They are then described as "professional misconduct." However unlike the other professions, those in ministry rarely receive training in their "professional ethics." A survey conducted by the survivors' group Friends of Susanna of ministerial training colleges in Australia and New Zealand found that none who responded had specific courses in professional ethics. Only recently has literature appeared on the topic, an example being the book *Sex in the Parish* by Lebacqz and Barton, which provides an ethical analysis of the power relationship operative in ministry and the ways in which sexual involvement exploits that power.

A breach in professional ethics is a serious matter. It is hard to imagine how ministry (or teaching, medicine or counseling for that matter) could operate if people felt that their wives, husbands, sons and daughters were not safe from sexual exploitation whenever they were left alone with a minister. Often people go to them at a time of vulnerability, seeking guidance and help. Ministry simply could not function if people did not feel safe going to their ministers.

Again, the actions of those who abuse the trust of people in their pastoral care can effectively undermine the whole ministry of the church as people lose confidence in the churches' appointed ministers.

Sadly most church authorities are not presently able to respond adequately to the issue at this level, except perhaps theoretically. They have not yet begun to use the theological resources of the Christian tradition to formulate a response or to reflect theologically on the nature of ministry. The responses have been limited to the sphere of ethics, not of faith.

## A VIOLATION OF THE NATURE OF MINISTRY

Ministers in Christian churches take on a special identification with the ministry of Jesus. A traditional theology of ministry speaks of the minister sharing in the priestly, prophetic and kingly mission of Jesus. Ministers lead the community in worship. They proclaim the Gospel in preaching. They provide the community with its pastoral leadership, organizing it as a Christian community of love and justice. In all this the minister is called to act as Jesus acted, sacrificing his/her own life (but not his/her integrity) to overcome the effects of evil in the world.[1] Indeed at the heart of the Catholic ordination ceremony is the command to "imitate in your own life

---

[1] In fact of course many ministers do sacrifice their integrity in trying to live up to the diverse expectations which congregations put onto them. This is not what a life of self-sacrifice is about. It is about the sacrifices one is called to make in order to maintain one's integrity.

the mystery you celebrate," that is to say, the eucharistic mystery of a life given in love to overcome evil.

Now it is clear that the ministry of Jesus was concerned with protecting the vulnerable and healing the wounded. For example, we find Jesus protecting the vulnerability of the woman caught in adultery and healing many of the walking wounded he encountered. Yet when ministers are sexually abusive, they exploit the vulnerable and add further injury to those already wounded. Indeed several survivors comment on how these ministers seem to have an almost uncanny ability to zero in upon vulnerable, wounded people (usually women and children). In so doing, they act in direct contrast to the way in which Jesus ministered.

Further, as pastors their task is to build up the Christian community through healing, forgiveness and encouragement. They are the bridge builders of the community, helping to resolve disputes and heal division. Yet when ministers act sexually and their actions become public, the result is invariably to introduce divisive forces within the community, forces which tear down and undermine it. In fact such actions defile its trust, the sacred trust of the whole Christian community in its leaders.

Finally, the Christian community seeks in its ministers moral and spiritual leadership. This does not mean one expects them to be morally and spiritually perfect, to be beyond reproach. This would be asking the impossible. Indeed ministers who project such an image should be suspected of self-delusion, and can be most prone to abusing others. Rather it means that ministers should be able to identify right from wrong, spiritual growth from spiritual decline, both in themselves and others. They should be able to realistically identify their own faults and limitations and humbly ask God for the grace to overcome them. As public figures their struggle becomes a public struggle for authenticity and integrity.[2]

Yet when ministers are in sexually abusive relationships they display a moral and spiritual bankruptcy which scandalizes the Christian community. The Christian community rightly expects

---

[2] Cf. Dorothy McRae-McMahon, *Being Clergy, Staying Human*, (Washington; An Alban Institute Publication, 1992).

greater personal integrity in its ministers. We need to be clear that sexually abusive relationships are often not the result of some moral struggle within the minister. Indeed he often does not see that he has done anything wrong, and can even rationalize his actions as somehow beneficial to his victims. Such a level of moral insensitivity is far more frightening than the plight of a minister involved in an intense moral struggle to do the right thing and failing in some way.[3]

Church leaders will begin to respond theologically to abusive ministers when they ask whether their sexually abusive actions do not so violate the nature of ministry as to require their dismissal. Such a dismissal would be a powerful public statement by church authorities that such actions are totally counter to the Christian message and the ministerial calling. They would be a clear indicator from church authorities that they are concerned with justice for survivors and not with protecting those in the "ministerial club."

Further, such a response is not an institutionalized lack of forgiveness, since it does not expel such people from the church, merely from ministry. It in fact is an offer of a real forgiveness which demands that the sinners seek to repair the damage they have done to their victims. Anything less than this minimizes the nature of the offence and hence makes of forgiveness an empty charade.

## SURVIVORS' EXPERIENCE OF THE RESPONSE OF CHURCH LEADERS

Analyzing the churches' response to disclosures of sexual abuse by ministers is one thing. How survivors experience that response is another. Survivors are on the receiving end of the churches' response and so are best placed to give the churches feedback, if they are willing to listen. Again, from the perspective of the survivors, these are the types of responses that occur.

---

[3] Lebacqz and Barton might describe such a minister as a "normal neurotic," cf. Chapter Four.

## 1. A preoccupation with false accusations

Among church authorities there is almost an obsessive concern with the possibility of false accusations. Indeed in the Catholic Church there are even canonical sanctions that can be imposed against someone who makes a false accusation against a priest (though there are no corresponding sanctions against a priest who makes a false denial!).[4] This concern with false accusations can mislead authorities so that they believe the denials and minimizations of perpetrators, without engaging in proper investigations. Further it should be noted that concern for false accusations has not led the churches to develop proper independent investigative procedures. Rather it is used to deflect serious attention to the issue of sexual abuse.

> In one case what was described by one church leader as a "thorough investigation" consisted of consulting a civil lawyer, a canon lawyer, a psychiatrist and a moral theologian. On the other hand no great interest was shown in gathering the actual facts of the case from survivors.

Further, there is a tendency among church authorities to see accused ministers as vindicated if claims do not withstand the rigors of the courtroom. Yet such legal vindication does not prove that the claims are false.

Far more likely than the making of false accusations will be the silent suffering of the victims as they struggle with their past abuse. Studies in the USA show that only four per cent of those abused by therapists ever take action. Figures in church situations are likely to be comparable.

## 2. Protecting the church legally and financially

It is clear from their response that a major concern of church leaders is the need to protect the churches financially and legally. Often the first person a church leader will contact is a lawyer. One major religious order in Australia responds to disclosures of sexual abuse by one of its priests by having a lawyer interview the survivor. No matter how well this is done or what the intentions

---

[4] Cf Canon 1390 of the *Code of Canon Law*.

are of those responsible, it is clearly sending the wrong signals to survivors, turning them into legal adversaries. The following is an account of how two survivors experienced this type of approach:

> We both wrote separately to the church official concerned. For a process that was to include pastoral care, we have been left feeling like "invisible women" and once again, our needs were negated.

> We were subjected to a legal process. This entailed meeting a lawyer (chosen by the male church official) to reveal the facts of our story. Apart from giving details of the abuse, we were questioned extensively and inappropriately about our backgrounds, our education, our family dynamics, even our personalities. It was an extremely intrusive procedure and we both felt that we were the ones "on trial." This legal procedure was a very rational one and excluded the pain, hurt and shame involved. Apart from the humiliation for us in having to answer so many questions, the lawyer involved in the investigation minimized some very painful details. We were left feeling unheard and negated. Although the lawyer tried to be sensitive, her minimization and her inadequate understanding of the issues involved in sexual abuse had a negative impact on us.

Eugene Kennedy has complained that church policies on the issue of sexual abuse are being driven by lawyers and insurance companies seeking to limit the churches' legal and financial liabilities.[5]

Of course such actions are counter-productive. Survivors are often not seeking legal and financial remedies to their sufferings. Rather they are seeking a pastoral response, one which acknowledges their suffering, the truthfulness of their claims and which calls the minister to account *within* the church. Instead church authorities tend to "un-name" the nature of what happened and treat survivors as invisible.[6] They fail to respond to letters or phone calls, or respond only briefly—the non-reply reply. They insulate themselves from the survivors by refusing them interviews

---

[5] Cf. Eugene Kennedy, "The see-no-problem, hear-no-problem, speak-no-problem problem," *National Catholic Reporter,* 19 March 1993, p.5.
[6] These are two characteristic ways in which the fallen angels operate in the book by Madeleine L'Engle, *A Wind In The Door* (New York; Dell Publishing, 1980).

and labeling them as vindictive, as interested only in compensation, as "disturbed" or as "feminists."

At the same time the abuse is "un-named." Pedophilia becomes "mutual masturbation," "love expressed inappropriately" or "moral indiscretions." Rape becomes "being a red-blooded male." Sexual harassment becomes "showing a bit of harmless affection." Pastoral sexual abuse of adult women becomes "being unfaithful to his celibacy," a "fault in his behavior," a "messy human situation" or simply an "affair." Even the term "sexual misconduct" does not express the damaging and relational nature of the behavior, that is the abuse of another person. It remains a euphemism. It's as though anything goes except naming the abuse for what it is, thus avoiding legal, moral or financial implications.

When survivors encounter legal obstacles or simply inaction from the churches, they will then seek legal advice as a last resort. If the church had responded adequately in the first place they might never have been so inclined. And of course when survivors seek legal remedies, they are then portrayed as "enemies of the church."

Worse, church leaders often try to silence survivors by accusing them of wanting retribution or wanting only compensation or of being partly to blame—"You were an adult, after all."

In the case of child sexual abuse, of course, the churches do have a serious cause for concern in that legal action and subsequent damages can be draining of church resources. Some US Catholic dioceses and religious orders are facing bankruptcy over sexual abuse settlements. Some estimate that the US Catholic church has paid out over $600 million in legal, out-of-court settlement and therapeutic costs. Yet this is the price the church must be willing to pay if it is to act as a morally responsible agent, and not simply attempt to protect its own financial interests. As Jesus reminds the churches, "Those who want to save their life will lose it" (Mark 8:35).

In the case of *adult* pastoral sexual abuse, some US States have passed statutes covering sexual abuse in the helping professions, and these have been seen as applying to abusive actions of ministers. In Australia, on the other hand, there is nothing like that. The legal situation in Australia at present is such that the churches seem to have little to fear. The best quasi-legal action that can be taken so far is to have ministers struck off various professional associations to which they may belong.

### 3. Protecting the church from scandal

A key value in church handling of disclosures of sexual abuse is that of protecting the church from scandal. This often means that a shroud of secrecy falls over the abusive minister. He simply drops out of sight, in the past simply moved to another pastoral setting, with no explanation ever given for his disappearance. It was vainly hoped that a new environment would produce a change in behavior.

Such actions invariably work for the perpetrator and against the survivor. For the perpetrator it creates an aura of sympathy on which he is able to play for his own advantage. Because no explanation is ever given, people imagine their own—sickness, the victim of arbitrary authority, the victim of unjust accusations and so on. Abusive ministers have shown themselves most capable of exploiting such an aura of sympathy. Because no public statement is ever made the survivors feel as if they have not been heard, that they are doubted or not taken seriously. This is part of the second round of abuse that many survivors experience.

While there is a place for confidentiality, uncritical confidentiality and secrecy may have greater negative consequences than an admission, particularly for survivors. The secrecy also compromises the integrity of the church as it fails to deal with evil in its ranks. Then from secrecy there is a short step to deception: self-deception and the deception of others. This is a phenomenon well known to survivors who make disclosures.

Again such actions are counter-productive. In their own way such actions are more scandalous for the churches, if and when they become public, than if they simply had the disclosures of sexual abuse alone to handle. The churches would be better served if they face such disclosures openly and frankly. In the long run this would be less damaging, both to the survivors, the perpetrators (in an ultimate sense) and the churches themselves.

### 4. No actual policy—What do you want us to do?

A most frightening response from church leaders to a survivor is the question "What do you want us to do?" While it might seem like a sensitive and compassionate question, it is often far more indicative of a lack of clearly defined and reflective policy on the part of the church. By pushing the matter back into the hands of the survivor, church leaders make them responsible for something which is really the church's responsibility. Survivors have had thrown at them comments such as, "He might commit suicide!" Typically if survivors do not pursue their case by harassing the responsible authorities (and hence being labeled vindictive for their trouble), nothing much happens.

Of course church authorities should listen to the needs of survivors and maintain dialogue with them, to keep them informed of what they are doing in relation to the perpetrator. But it is the authorities' responsibility to handle the situation, one they cannot throw back onto the survivor.

To this end churches should have clearly defined policies and expected outcomes in place whenever disclosures of sexual abuse are made. These policies should not depend on survivors pursuing the matter, often forced to act as advocates for their own case. This is a very common situation for survivors to find themselves in and indicates that church leaders have not thought out their policies clearly—in fact many have no real policy at all for dealing with disclosures.

## THE CHURCH AS INCESTUOUS FAMILY

The experience of survivors of sexual abuse when they come forward with disclosures of abuse is not dissimilar to the experience of many incest victims when they break their silence and inform their family.

Indeed in popular theological rhetoric, church communities are often likened to the family. In some denominations the family symbolism is reinforced by giving ministers the title of "Father." Even where this is not the case, the minister who becomes sexually involved with those in his pastoral care has the power of a trusted father figure who violates the sexual boundary of vulnerable people in order to satisfy his own sexual or other intrapsychic compulsions. Unfortunately, the analogy with the incestuous family continues to hold true when victims finally decide to break the "family secret."

We would now like to explore the analogy in more detail.

### * Church structures

One of the most accurate predictors of possible incest in a family is the presence of authoritarian and/or patriarchal power relationships [7]. These are precisely the types of relationships fostered in many churches, from the strictly hierarchical churches to the least structured house churches. In church communities the minister is *the* most influential person, often to the point of having absolute authority, whether that authority is based on his sacramental role or his role as interpreter of the Scriptures for his community. Most churches remain male dominated in their authority structures, either on traditional or Scriptural grounds.

### * The offender

By seeking to satisfy his inner compulsions, the offending minister is like the incestuous parent who inverts the normal roles of caregiver and child. The offender seeks nurturing from the person in his pastoral care, and is at the same time grossly insensitive to the victim's needs. Typically he will deceive himself that he is "showing affection," that this is "love" ... "He has little or no sense of conscience about his offending behaviors. He usually will minimize, lie and deny when confronted."[8]

### * The "no-talk rule"

The unhealthy dynamics of the incestuous family become most obvious when victims approach church authorities with disclosures of misconduct. Here the "no-talk rule" of unhealthy, dysfunctional families is broken. All too often church authorities react as mothers do to a child's report of incest. Eugene Kennedy has spoken of this as the "See-no-problem, Hear-no-problem, Speak-no-problem Problem."[9]

---

[7] George Thorman notes that where incest occurs, "studies indicate that power is highly concentrated in the father and that he holds a dominant position in families," *Incestuous Families*, (Chicago; Charles C. Thomas, 1983).

[8] Cf. Fortune, p.47.

[9] Cf. E. Kennedy, op. cit.

### * Scapegoating

Incestuous families are characteristically preoccupied with projecting a nearly perfect image to outsiders, while tolerating unacceptable behavior on the inside. When the unacceptable behavior is exposed by the victimized member, the family will avoid taking responsibility by finding a scapegoat—often the victim. The family attempts to convince the questioning family member that the incest is not the problem, but rather that he or she is the problem for breaking the "no-talk rule."

Survivors or their parents who come to church authorities with disclosures will recognize these dynamics easily. They discover, to their deep disappointment, that the authorities treat them as adversaries, not as people who have been hurt and who are in need of pastoral care.

## A MAJOR DIFFICULTY

The greatest difficulty which church leaders need to face in dealing with sexual abuse is in themselves. The person who stands accused before them is a minister like themselves, often personally known to them, someone with whom they have shared experiences and a common church culture. It is to be expected that church leaders will experience a spontaneous identification with the perpetrator, to feel sorry for him, to appreciate the pressures he has been under and so on. They will also have shared a common tradition of warnings about "seductive, manipulative women." This is a form of counter-transference, which seduces the church leader into colluding with the abusive minister in his denial and minimization of his actions. It is of course the old problem of "who guards the guards?"

At worst, the identification with the perpetrator is complete when the church leader himself is a perpetrator, as happens all too frequently. Archbishop Robert Sanchez of New Mexico was forced to resign when five women came forward with allegations that he had had sexual relations with them. Previously he had been criticized for responding ineffectually to complaints of child sexual abuse.[10]

---

[10] *NCR*, 19 March 1993, p.5.

In Catholicism the situation is made more difficult because of the discipline of priestly celibacy. It is likely that most priests experience at some time in their ministry a real test for their celibacy. They feel attracted to a woman in their pastoral care, may even become romantically involved and so are forced into a crisis in their vocation—should they leave the priesthood and marry, or recommit themselves to celibacy and continue in ministry? When a priest is then required to confront or discipline a fellow priest who has been acting out sexually, he may spontaneously project his own time of testing onto the priest before him, no matter how inappropriate such projection may be. The result is that the church leader becomes unable to respond adequately to the abusive priest.

In Protestant churches a parallel problem arises. Many Protestant ministers enter ministry unmarried but fairly quickly find a suitable marriage partner from within one of their first congregations.[11] This has been seen as both normal and appropriate. Yet the analysis which we and others, such as Lebacqz and Barton, have put forward would question the ethics of such a procedure. Of course such a courtship may fall into the category of the "normal neurotic" and given it is in the public arena and there is a commitment on the part of the minister to equalize power in the relationship it may be acceptable. However, again, when a Protestant minister is required to confront a fellow minister who has been acting out sexually he too can project his own experience of courtship and marriage, no matter how inappropriate such projection may be. The result is that the church leader becomes unable to respond adequately to the abusive minister.

## PASTORAL CARE

These problems add up to bad news for survivors who seek some form of justice from church leaders. Not only is justice lacking but often so is pastoral care. Survivors are treated as legal adversaries, as institutional threats. Often the survivors are dealing with their

---

[11] Acknowledgments to Rev. Patricia Allen who made this point in her presentation at the "Project Anna" seminar, Melbourne, November, 1993.

own difficulties in facing up to the effects of their abuse, such as post-traumatic shock disorder. They are hurting and deeply wounded. Yet far from receiving pastoral care they are put at arm's length and treated as enemies. If they are lucky they may receive an offer of money to pay for future (but rarely past) therapy.[12] Church leaders are slow to return phone calls or respond to letters. Survivors never really know where they as survivors stand, nor where the church leader stands. All this adds to the already painful burden which the survivor is asked to carry.

Yet while the pastoral care of survivors is minimal, often the pastoral care of abusive ministers is equally lacking. A minister who has to face a history of sexual abusive activities can be thrown into a deep personal crisis. The intervention of church leaders may result in a breakdown in the various rationalizations and minimizations which he has used to conceal the nature of the activities even from himself. This is a shattering experience which can lead at best to serious psychological confusion and at worst to a suicidal despair. Yet often they find themselves in such a state with little direct care and support. Here again the minimization of events on the part of church leaders does not even help the perpetrator for it fails to recognize the depth of the crisis that the perpetrator may have been forced to enter.

> When one survivor asked how her perpetrator was faring after disclosures had been made against him the person in charge of his pastoral care said he didn't know, as he had not seen him for three weeks. This was at the height of the perpetrator's personal crisis.

All this is indicative of a lack of resources being put into facing the problem of sexual abuse by ministers. More resources are needed in the development of policy, in providing pastoral care for survivors and for perpetrators. Until such resources are made available the church will not be seen to be taking the problem seriously.

---

[12] Such an offer is a double-edged sword since it tends to pathologize the victim—"see, they are really the problem"—rather than address the question of justice.

## PRINCIPLES FOR AN AUTHENTIC RESPONSE[13]

It is not our intention here to recommend detailed mechanisms for an authentic response on the part of church leaders. However, we would like to put forward the principles on which such a response could be based and what they might mean. These would be equally applicable whether the person was abused as an adult or as a child.

In discussing these principles what we are calling for, as much as anything, is a change of heart on the part of those whose duty it is to respond to disclosures. Good policies and procedures are important, but without a genuine and active commitment to certain values the gross injustices of the current situation will continue.

### * Preferential option for the poor

Scripture informs us of God's particular concern for victims of oppression, wounded, vulnerable or marginalized people. Jesus' identification with victims was so total he eventually met their fate. This is not to say that perpetrators are not victims themselves. In all likelihood they are. But in this sphere of their lives they must clearly be seen as perpetrators of great harm.

This preferential option for the poor has two dimensions. Firstly it implies that survivors of abuse should have the first call on the compassion and resources of the churches. Secondly survivors are in a position of "hermeneutic privilege"; that is to say their perspective on events should carry considerably more weight than that of their abusers.[14]

### * Commitment to truth and integrity

This principle has various dimensions.

Commitment to this principle means breaking through denial. Church leaders are challenged to become educated about the issue, for example, about the effects of sexual abuse on victims, and to acknowledge publicly the seriousness and extent of the sexual abuse problem.

---

[13] See also, Fortune, pp.108–129.
[14] These are two key insights that have emerged from Liberation Theology.

Commitment to truth and integrity also means a definition of "sexual abuse" which is more inclusive than that which is contained in secular law in many places. Sexual abuse occurs when there is any eroticizing of a pastoral relationship, be it with a child or an adult, leading to damage in the less powerful person. The moral standards of the churches should surely be higher than the minimums enshrined in criminal law.

In addition, because of the profound and life-long damage that results from sexual abuse, there should be no "statute of limitations." Commonly the abuse is repressed for long periods, even decades, so survivors need to be free to move in their own time.

Commitment to truth and integrity means setting up thorough and independent investigative processes. It is unrealistic to think that fellow clergy will make truly objective judgments on, say, a panel of investigation. Moreover the findings and disciplinary determinations of an independent panel of investigation should not be open to modification by church leaders.

The panel should be assisted by an independent professional investigator. It is not good enough for the responsible people to "ask around." And certainly it cannot be assumed that an accused clergyman is telling the truth when he gives his testimony.

A professional investigator can test the validity of specific claims and discover if there are other victims. Because of the frequency of one perpetrator abusing a number of people and the fact that only a minority of survivors come forward to complain, it is quite possible that a single complaint represents the "tip of the iceberg."

Also the investigation should proceed even if the complaint is withdrawn. Because complainants are often subject to pressure from family, friends or clergy, it is not unusual for complaints to be withdrawn before an investigation is completed.

## * Compassion for survivors

It is most important that complaints are received by someone who is able to show sensitivity and concern. A trained sexual assault counselor, a woman, should be the first point of contact, someone who can process the complaint and provide pastoral support and advocacy. The response at this point should be immediate, and care should be taken throughout to respond speedily to victims'/ survivors' letters or requests.

Free counseling through the church's counseling agency should be offered as an option, as well as full cover for the costs of private therapy. Costs of past therapy should be reimbursed.

Complainants need as much information as possible regarding the process of dealing with their disclosures. They need to know what grievance procedure will be followed, and to be kept informed of how the case is progressing. It is generally safe to assume complainants want to know. They should not have to ask for such information.

Often survivors come forward after many years of silence so they have a great need to be heard. They need acknowledgment for the pain they have suffered and respect for the way they hope their disclosures will be handled.

### * Needs of ministers said to have offended

In justice church authorities are concerned about the reputation of the minister involved, in case claims made against them prove to be unfounded. However the likelihood of false claims is far lower than the actual rates of abuse. Those who make claims realize how exposed they make themselves. It takes real courage for a survivor, usually already burdened with self-blame and shame, to make a disclosure of abuse, so the presumption should be that the situation deserves serious attention.

Nonetheless, the rights to natural justice of those accused must be respected. They have the right to be heard, the right to confidentiality, to be considered innocent until found guilty. They also need good pastoral care and the option of counseling support for the period in which they are removed from ministry and investigations are in progress.

If they are found to be perpetrators they will need specialist counseling to come to grips with their past. This involves challenging their habits of self-deception and confronting them with the consequences of their actions as well as supporting them in facing any abuse in their own childhood which predisposed them to becoming abusers.

## *Justice for survivors*

Survivors are likely to need an advocate to represent their interests to any investigation panel. It is extraordinarily difficult for a person to act as their own advocate in matters which are so painful.

When the investigation comes to a conclusion as to the nature and extent of the violation, this should be acknowledged and an apology offered in writing. If a church finds itself with the case of a minister who has used his structural power for sexual purposes it must clearly name this as sexual abuse. Sexual assault should likewise be named as such.

Restitution is integral to justice and cannot truthfully be seen as the responsibility only of the perpetrator. As institutions, churches are responsible for providing adequate training and structures of accountability to prevent major abuses of power. Also, it is because churches endorse certain people as being worthy of trust that these people have the power to do harm.

An open-ended offer of restitution should be made in writing. The form of restitution should be chosen to some extent by the survivor. It could be a public apology. It could involve reimbursement of medical and legal expenses as well as compensation for pain and suffering.

It is important here to distinguish between the need to respect the wishes of survivors and the danger of making them responsible for the conduct of the case. Once the allegations have been substantiated, the church has the responsibility to make an authentic response without further burdening survivors.

Justice requires that the perpetrator should not be assisted in evading the truth of his actions. He should remain out of ministry while he is helped to come to the point of acknowledging the full reality of the harm he has done and accepting responsibility for his behavior. Where this does not eventuate or if the violation of trust is very serious, justice requires that the perpetrator be taken out of ministry indefinitely. This is not to say he no longer belongs in the church. It is to say he has forfeited his entitlement to the privileged and trusted position of minister.

Finally, survivors' right to seek redress through the legal system should be acknowledged. Church authorities should cooperate fully with this process.

### * Restitution before forgiveness

Some churches are developing processes heavily influenced by the ideals of forgiveness and reconciliation. It must be understood that any pressure to forgive is detrimental to the healing process in the victim/survivor. Victims need to feel the full extent of their anger and pain before they can come to the point where they may be free to forgive. Even then it can only be hoped for as a gift.

Another problem with reconciliation as a goal is that it tends to ignore the fact that one party is less powerful socially and has been victimized. These are not matters for mediation between two equals where the goals are clearer communication and mutually agreeable outcomes. We would not consider instigating such a process between a thief and the thief's victim!

Almost invariably the perpetrator will deny or minimize the significance of his actions. Until he acknowledges fully the hurt he has caused and sincerely accepts responsibility for it, until reparation is offered, any expectation of forgiveness or reconciliation adds further to the injustice.

### * Healing the community

The local church community within which the events took place will include within it many secondary victims. Their trust has also been betrayed, causing shocked disbelief, grief, feelings of betrayal and helplessness and crises of faith. There be attempts to maintain normalcy at all costs. Some people will deal with their feelings by blaming the victim.

The community deserves a formal response from church authorities. This could include an apology and an opportunity to work through feelings with the assistance of someone with expertise.

### * Protecting the church

Structures need to be put in place which serve to protect the vulnerable from exploitation. Structures of accountability would also mean that believers in general are more able to be confident their ministers will act with integrity.

All clergy should sign a code of ethics which precludes sexualized contact with those in their care. This code should define behavior which will lead to permanent removal from ministry. Lay people should be made aware of the code.

There needs to be careful screening of applicants for ministry, and training in the dynamics of pastoral relationships and their theological implications. Those already in ministry should be required to attend in-service training in these areas.

Clergy need to develop practices which will safeguard them and those they pastor. Supervision and peer support are crucial.

All clergy ought to be bound to pass on complaints or concerns they have about other ministers' behavior. Failure to do so should lead to serious disciplinary action. Senior clergy ought to be bound to follow a comprehensive protocol when dealing with complaints.

All church members need to be aware of the possibilities of abuse in the same way that patients need to be aware of their rights to professional medical care. It is important that there be a widespread understanding that complaints will be received sympathetically and taken seriously. Protocol documents should be publicly available.

The culture of tolerance of sexual abuse needs to be openly challenged from the pulpit and through education. It is silence about the issue which enables this injustice to continue. Ministers in particular and men in general who act as though they are entitled to sexual favors from those placed in their care should no longer receive the protection society affords them.

## CONCLUSION: A BISHOP'S RESPONSIBILITY

The Greek term *episkopos* from which we derive the term "bishop," means overseer. One aspect of the ministry of the bishop, or its equivalent, is to oversee the actions of the church's ministers. Yet given the size of many church structures there is no effective supervision of ministers once they are ordained. Some minimal psychological screening occurs before and during training, yet once a person is ordained or installed there is little practical follow-up. There are no effective structures of accountability within most churches.

All the churches need to develop an effective ministry of over-seeing those in ministry, someone with the spiritual authority needed to break through denial, to confront minimization, to call the minister to account. However this is often not enough. Bishops come from the same culture as the perpetrator, they identify with him, and in some cases, as we have already observed, may be perpetrators themselves. Effective structures of accountability need to be two-way, allowing communication to flow in both directions, from people to ministers and bishops and back again. Those in ministry must be able to give an account of their ministry to the people they serve, and to be called to account by them. Until such structures exist sexual abuse and other forms of the abuse of power will remain ingrained within church cultures. We shall consider this further in the next chapter.

Church authorities must honor their mandate to serve the needs of their believers/members, particularly those who are wounded or vulnerable. In the words of the Presbyterian Church (USA) policy:

> We are facing a crisis terrible in its proportions and implications ...
> In a context of trust it is hard to recognize abusive behavior because we do not expect to see it. In fact, as in families where incest occurs, we may find that we have chosen not to see. When that occurs we, too, are complicit. Now that our consciousness is raised, we are responsible for appropriate intervention and prevention ... The integrity of the denomination and its ministry is at stake.

# CHAPTER SIX

# A "THEOLOGY" OF ABUSE—JUSTIFYING THE UNJUSTIFIABLE

Sexual abuse is one symptom, perhaps the worst symptom, of a much wider abuse of power within the churches. From fundamentalist churches to the hierarchical sacramental ones, there are patterns of abuse to which divine sanction is ascribed. In this chapter we move attention from sexual abuse alone to consider the ways in which religious faith can be distorted by a more general abuse of power.

## ABUSE AND THE CHURCHES

Physical, psychological and sexual abuse are among the most destructive forces present in society. The victims of the most severe abuse fill our prisons and commit the most heinous of crimes, rape, serial murder and so on. One survey has revealed that 90 per cent of inmates in US prisons admit to having a history of abuse. Psychologist Alice Miller comments "the remaining ten per cent were not yet able to admit it".[1] Those less affected live a life of damaged self-esteem, acting out a variety of strategies to recover what abuse has stolen from them. Indeed in some way or other we have all suffered, all had our original sense of worth and dignity stolen from us, through the actions of either our parents or other powerful people in our lives.[2]

---

[1] Alice Miller, *Banished Knowledge*, pp.27–8.
[2] See Neil Ormerod, *Grace and Disgrace*, pp.23-6, for a fuller exposition of this dynamic.

Given the destructiveness of such forces, given the damage they do both psychologically and spiritually, one would expect the churches to be speaking out on the issue of abuse as a simple matter of course. Yet too often the voices of the churches are silent. Indeed the inculcation of "faith" has itself often been abusive, filling believers with fears of punishment, temporal or eternal, if they do not continue to be "good Christians." Despite the almost epidemic levels of child abuse in society and in church communities, the churches remain silent, even when abuse is found to be perpetrated by their own ministers.

Behind the silence is a theology (or, more correctly, an ideology) which has frequently provided an unconscious justification for abuse. Key narratives and doctrines of the Christian faith have been portrayed as providing subtle justifications for what are destructive relationships in situations of power imbalance, typically the parent–child relationship and those modeled on this relationship, for example the minister and his congregant. In fact this portrayal is nothing more than a perversion of the Christian faith, a distortion which turns true faith on its head. As such it goes far beyond the advice to "spare the rod and spoil the child" and turns Christianity into its negative image by justifying the unjustifiable.

## THE STORY OF ISAAC—A PARABLE OF ABUSE[3]

God said "Take your son, your only son Isaac, whom you love, and go to the land of Moriah, and offer him as a burnt offering on one of the mountains that I shall show you". (Genesis 22:2)

The story of Abraham and Isaac is one of the better known biblical stories, but also one of the most readily misunderstood. On a first reading the story seems very strange. Abraham and Sarah had been childless, despite God's promise that they would be the parents of a great nation. Abraham tries first to force God's

---

[3] We are aware that this is a very "Catholic" reading of the text. Protestant exegesis has been influenced by Soren Kierkegaard, via Karl Barth, and tends to place more emphasis on the blind "leap of faith". For an alternative reading of the Isaac story, see James Newton Poling, pp.158ff.

hand by taking a concubine and fathering Ishmael, but Sarah eventually conceives and bears the child, Isaac. Isaac is the beloved son, the one whom God seems to have destined to carry on Abraham's lineage. Yet the next thing we hear is that God wants Abraham to sacrifice Isaac as a burnt offering. At the very least God seems a bit confused about what he is trying to achieve!

Without a moment's hesitation Abraham prepares a donkey for the journey and takes off to the mountain to kill his son. He is only prevented from slaughtering his child by the timely intervention of an angel of Yahweh. Unbeknown to Abraham the whole thing has been a test of his faith. He has proved faithful, done what God has wanted without hesitation. He has won God's approval:

> ... because you have done this, and have not withheld your son, your only son, I will indeed bless you, and I will make your offspring as numerous as the stars of heaven ... (Genesis 22:16–17)

From this point on Abraham becomes a model of faith. God has put him to the test and he has proved faithful, an interpretation which even finds its way into the New Testament (cf. Hebrews 11:17ff).

Yet there is something radically wrong with this whole picture. The strangeness and inconsistency of God's position is evident, and only marginally eased by being placed in the context of a "test of faith." What is really going on in this story?

## TEST OF FAITH OR COMPULSIVE FANATICISM?

The first thing that needs to be clearly said is that Abraham is wrong to undertake to kill his son. Such an act of ritual sacrifice is totally immoral under any circumstances. No command believed to be from God can make it right. Nothing can make right wrong and wrong right. (Of course one could say God is only testing Abraham, but then that would mean that God is deliberately deceiving him, which is also unacceptable.)

What we are seeing in Abraham's behavior is not an act of religious faith but an act of compulsive religious fanaticism. If we believe that God can command us to do a morally evil act then really we can justify anything. The outcome of such a position is not religious faith but religious fanaticism. "It is the will of God/Allah/Vishnu/Yahweh" is the constant cry of the religious fanatic down through the ages. The picture of such fanaticism has scarred human history far too deeply and continues to do so wherever religion is used as a rationalization of inhumane acts of cruelty and destruction.[4]

As a test of faith, Abraham's initial response fails since he has not listened to the deeper law written in his heart, but has acted out of a compulsive religious fanaticism which has blinded him to the truth.

Indeed biblical scholars now recognize more fully the significance of the Isaac story. The story arises out of a culture in which child sacrifice (of the first born) was not uncommon and was indeed seen by some as a religious obligation. However it is not the voice of Yahweh that Abraham hears telling him to sacrifice his son, but rather the voice of Canaanite fertility cults and their idols.[5] The intervention of the angel of Yahweh then symbolizes a complete rejection of these fertility cults. In its original context the story amounts to a polemic against child sacrifice—God does not want the sacrifice of Isaac, God does not want the sacrifice of any child. Abraham finds faith when he listens to God and turns away from sacrificing his son.

Sadly, however, the context shifted and the original story became less intelligible as it was passed down in the oral tradition, perhaps because of the suppression of the memory of such horrific child sacrifices. Seeking to revive the story the tradition itself reinterpreted the story as one of a test of faith. While of some value, this reinterpretation takes the sharp edge off the telling point being made in the original context. More than that in fact, because it helps hide and so subverts the original context.

---

[4] See also Alice Miller on "female circumcision" as a horrific example of "repetition compulsion" given religious justification, *Breaking Down the Wall of Silence*, pp.75ff.

[5] Roland de Vaux, *Ancient Israel*, (London; Darton, Longman and Todd, 1961) pp.443–6.

## THE CHRISTIAN STORY

No Christian can read the story of Abraham and Isaac without sensing the deep resonance with the story of Jesus. Abraham must sacrifice his beloved son. Echoing this the New Testament speaks of God sending his only beloved Son to die for our sins. Indeed the theological tradition, drawing on the Letter to the Hebrews speaks of Jesus' death as a sacrifice, the sacrifice of the only beloved son. Further within the Abraham and Isaac story, Abraham speaks the "prophetic" words, "God himself will provide the sacrifice," (cf. Genesis 22:7). Jesus is then the one who is sacrificed in Isaac's place and indeed in the place of us all.

In fact one does not have to look far to find people speaking of the death of Jesus on the cross as a sacrifice to appease the anger of God. Jesus dies on the cross because that is what God wants of him as an act of filial obedience, to suffer in the place of a sinful humanity. "The son of man *must* die" for this is the will of God.

Read thus, the story becomes little more than a theological justification for abuse of the divine child. The anger of the Father (read: the anger of the parent) is vented on the innocent divine child. The child has done nothing to deserve this punishment, indeed nothing could deserve such a cruel punishment. Jesus is openly acknowledged as sinless, a pure and innocent sacrifice. Finally, to round off the logic of abuse, the child is told that in this punishment he/she is beloved, that the punishment is really "God's will," that the parent is really loving the child in inflicting the abuse. And in all this the child is asked to accept in silent obedience, suffering the anger of God/parent in sacrificial passivity.

Something must be wrong with such a pattern of thought. Does God really want Jesus to suffer and die on the cross? Is this really the will of God? Or are we missing the point, just as the biblical editor missed the point of the Abraham and Isaac story and turned it into a test of faith?

The first thing again that needs to be said is that the death of Jesus on the cross, the death of the innocent person, is a grave injustice, a terrible evil and hence wrong. God cannot will an evil act, God cannot turn an evil act into a good act or vice versa (though God may of course draw good out of evil). It cannot be said often enough or loudly enough, God did not will the death of Jesus on the cross. If this is how we understand the story of Jesus then we can justify any evil—if God can will such an evil act then God can will us to do evil acts, such as the bombing of Hiroshima, political terrorism, murder, rape and suicide. All these would be valid because "God told me to do it." Such a god is nothing more than the demonic in disguise.

Jesus dies not because it is the will of God, but because of the evil in the hearts of those who put him to death. Such evil is not the will of God. Though he dies because of his fidelity to God's mission, in confronting the evil of his day, in confronting the religious leaders with their hypocrisy and self-righteousness, it is evil in the heart of men and women that leads to his death. The death of Jesus is not "necessary" because it is God's will. It is necessary because of the hardness of heart of humanity, which refuses to hear the message of God's mercy and love. It is the religious leaders of the day who sacrifice Jesus. He was too inconvenient, too different, too challenging, too good for them to handle.

Indeed, like Abraham, the religious leaders thought they were doing God's will in having Jesus killed. They saw him as a blasphemer, someone who was threatening the religious order of the day. It was better for him to die, indeed it was "God's will" that he die, rather than change that sacred religious order. They showed themselves willing to sacrifice anyone who stood in the way of their sacred vision of things. Unlike the story of Abraham and Isaac there is no happy ending in the story of Jesus, no angel sent to prevent the final filial sacrifice. The story of Jesus is history, not legend; the outcome is all too realistic, too predictable—a painful, apparently meaningless death on the cross.

## THE LOGIC OF EVIL

What lies at the heart of the story of Jesus is the logic of evil. It is the logic which is willing to sacrifice anyone or anything which stands in the way of some perceived good. It is the logic which clearly sees ends and will use any means to achieve them. It is the logic of willingly doing evil, in order to achieve an apparently good end. It is a logic which blinds itself to the suffering it causes lest it be forced to change its ways. The higher the good, particularly a religious good, the more willing people are to sacrifice anything to achieve it.

Such a vision does not see the realm of values as an integral whole, where means must match ends, where lower goods can be preserved, respected and valued even while higher goods are sought. Rather it fragments the good into disjointed packages, into a series of either/or propositions, of stark alternatives. Then to choose one is to sacrifice the other, to reject and even vilify the other, finally to see what is really good as evil.[6]

This was the situation that the religious leaders in Jesus' day found themselves in. Jesus was offering a new religious vision, an opportunity to heal the divisions between rich and poor, Gentile and Jew, male and female, sinner and righteous. Such a vision did not negate the old religious vision of the Jewish faith. Rather it brought it to its proper completion. Jesus was not denying the validity of the old order, he was not denying its value. Yet to the religious leaders it had become an either/or situation. To them, accepting the new vision necessarily meant a denial of the value of the old, the religious order that they held dear and which justified their existence! Nothing was going to stand in the way of their hold on that old religious order and so Jesus must be sacrificed, according to the "law of God," according to the sacred order they loved and which also justified their special status.

Jesus became a victim to the logic of evil. The good that he offered was sacrificed in order to maintain a religious status quo. Given the high nature of the good being protected—indeed it was a sacred value—any sacrifice could be and was justified in their eyes.

---

[6] See for example, Rosemary Haughton's notion of exchange, *The Passionate God*, (London; Darton, Longman and Todd, 1981), pp.18ff.

## THE DOCTRINE OF ORIGINAL SIN—A CHARTER FOR ABUSE?[7]

Another element in the Christian tradition which can operate so as to justify abuse is the doctrine of original sin. To most people, not familiar with theological subtlety, the doctrine of original sin simply means "we're all born bad," we are sinners from the moment of our birth (some would even say from our conception). We have within us an inclination to sin which somehow we have to deal with, or we will turn out even worse sinners. Indeed, Augustine, the father of the doctrine of original sin, could argue in his spiritual classic, *The Confessions*, that the crying of babies is evidence of their sinfulness. He states:

> What sins then did I commit when I was a baby myself? Was it a sin to cry when I wanted to feed at the breast? ... I deserved a scolding for what I did; but since I could not have understood the scolding, it would have been unreasonable and most unusual to rebuke me ... It can hardly be right for a child, even at that age, to cry for everything ... (*Confessions*, Book 1, Ch.7)

Further, while Catholic theology saw the guilt of original sin removed by baptism, the Reformers felt that even baptism was not enough, that the human being remained basically corrupt.

How do you treat a child that you see as basically "bad" or at best "inclined towards sin"? It is most unlikely that you will simply accept the child's natural inclinations as good or at best neutral. Rather they are suspect, they need shaping, training, discipline and if they do not respond then they may need to be beaten out of the child, for the child's own good, of course. The child's will "must be broken" so that it can become submissive and obedient. If the child resists or becomes angry at such treatment, this is simply a further sign of its basic badness and the punishment will need to be increased proportionately to make sure it learns its lesson.

Of course the psychological evidence is that far from beating evil out of a child, evil is beaten into it by such treatment. The unequivocal evidence is that such abuse damages the child's

---

[7] For a more full account of the doctrine of original sin see Ormerod's *Grace and Disgrace*, pp.87–195.

self-esteem, its sense of dignity, and can lead the child to a life of perpetuating cycles of violence upon further helpless victims or turning its violence in upon itself, leading to self-hatred or, worse still, suicide.

But what if the doctrine of original sin is not saying that the child is "born bad," rather it becomes bad by the abusive, sinful actions of those around it? What if baptism of the child is a way of saying, "You don't need to beat the evil out of your child (a evil which is simply a projection of your own sinfulness), rather God declares this child just and pure through the waters of baptism"? Would we not again have turned a "traditional" position on its head?

## MISSING THE POINT

In the story of Abraham and Isaac we have stated that the biblical editor missed the original point and turned it into one of a test of faith. Similarly, in the Jesus story, our theologies have turned it from an account of evil sacrificing Jesus in order to protect a sacred order, into an account of the Father sacrificing his only beloved Son in order to appease the divine anger. To do this is to miss the point. However it is not to miss the point in some random fashion, as if the pieces of the puzzle have been thrown in the air to see where they land. Rather they miss the point in a very systematic way. The story is not only misunderstood, it is subverted. Rather than seeing the story of Abraham and Isaac as a rejection of the very possibility of child sacrifice, it has been turned into a test of faith in which God can indeed rightly ask for Isaac to be sacrificed. Rather than see Jesus' death and resurrection as a divine protest at the logic of evil which is willing to sacrifice an innocent man, it has become a story of Jesus needing to be sacrificed in order to appease the divine anger.

Why are we so willing to turn such stories around, to miss their point in such a perverse fashion? Why do we find such a perversion so believable?

In a remarkable series of works, psychotherapist Alice Miller has given evidence of the persistent inability of people to come to terms with childhood abuse because of their inability to blame the parent figure for any wrongdoing. People will consistently find excuses for even quite brutal parental abuse: "I deserved it," "They were only doing what they thought best," "They were going through a difficult time." Parents were justified or at least excused for their abusive behavior. They were right to sacrifice the child in their moment of anger. Once we accept such a logic the consequence that immediately follows is: "We too are justified in sacrificing those over whom we have power."

This is the ingrained nature of what the tradition calls "original sin." The logic of evil is passed on from generation to generation as a form of repetition compulsion. So ingrained is this logic of sin that we are even willing to see it operating in the divine sphere so that God himself becomes an abusive father willing to sacrifice his only son to the divine anger. We accept such a theological account because it so well fits the logic of the world, the logic of abuse from which, in some way, we all suffer.

## THE ABUSE OF POWER IN THE CHURCHES

Abuse is not only a problem in the churches, of course, but it is a special problem for the churches. Sexual abuse, which has been the focus of this book, is just one aspect, one dimension, one symptom of a much wider problem. Ministers are persons of power. In hierarchical churches this power can be almost absolute, with no real structures of accountability present at all. For example, a priest in his parish is accountable to no-one in that parish. A bishop in the diocese is accountable to no-one in his diocese. All the accountability structures work from above, not below. And even those which do work from above are often ineffectual. We have already considered this in the previous chapter.

However even in non-hierarchical churches, the church minister or leader can and does attract considerable structural power. He is a man of God, preacher of God's word from the Scriptures. To question him, to challenge his authority, is to challenge God's own authority. He can make a claim to be the authoritative interpreter of God's will for his community, and once such a claim is made, who could stand in his way? Such a claim to absolute authority is perhaps unparalleled in the secular world apart from totalitarian regimes.

When people have power, particularly when there is no real accountability, then abuse is almost inevitable. As Michael Novak comments:

> Even philosopher kings, given total power, may sooner or later be tempted to torture others—for their own good, for state [or church?] security, for the common good.[8]

While church ministers may not have the power to torture (any more!), they do have a spiritual power over their congregations, power which it is very easy to abuse. Few of them are trained in the exercise of that power, or taught the professional responsibilities associated with that power. Fewer of them are aware enough of their own brokenness to know the inner dynamics that will compel them to abusive actions when coming face to face with the vulnerability of another.

The situation is made more complex because the minister will often not feel himself to be very powerful personally. He may in fact feel powerless, alienated, and frustrated. Ministry is rarely a rewarding career option. However this disparity between the actual (structural) power that the minister has and the powerlessness he feels can in fact be the seed-bed of abuse. In the frustration that he feels he may begin to act out in irresponsible ways, unaware of the damage he does with the real structural power he possesses. Abusive ministers rarely see themselves as personally powerful people. The power of ministry becomes a compensation for what they lack personally.

Again it must be stressed that abuse of power rarely occurs as the result of a deliberate decision, where the minister is aware of his own power and the vulnerability of the other. If only it were that simple! No, abuse most commonly is not intentional, not something which is intended to harm and can even be thought to be "for the good" of the person being abused. Indeed the most abusive ministers are paternalistic and patronizing, sure that they know what is for your good and totally unable to listen to your individual story of suffering and vulnerability. In all likelihood such ministers are acting out a pattern of behavior imposed on

---

[8] Michael Novak, *Will it Liberate?*, (Paulist Press, 1986) pp.200–201.

them as children, or during their training, when their own suffering and vulnerability was not acknowledged.

Abusive behaviors come in many varieties. In this book we have focused on the issue of sexual abuse. But there are many different forms of abuse of power. Ministers can be abusive of whole congregations. Since they are in charge of liturgical celebrations, they have a number of opportunities to abuse power, particularly through sermons which berate the congregation, or which are ill-prepared and rambling, or which are simply a moralizing barrage of "shoulds." They can "use the Lord's name in vain" by ascribing divine assent to their own idiosyncratic views of the faith or the world. They can shield themselves from legitimate criticism by invoking ministerial privileges.

As leaders of their communities they can engage in autocratic decision making, failing to consult those who are affected by their decisions, or to be sensitive to their needs and legitimate aspirations. And of course they will blame their congregations when things go wrong. To make things worse all these things can be done with the absolute conviction that they are "for the good of the community/person" involved. Of course such convictions can be found in the most brutal of totalitarian regimes.[9] Ministers can also be abusive towards individuals by failing to listen to the experience of congregants with whom they are in conflict, by blaming them for any and every aspect of the dispute and most commonly by simply refusing to dialogue.

Yet actions which fail to attend to the suffering of the less powerful, the ones at the receiving end of these "good intentions," are invariably abusive.

One survivor of pastoral sexual abuse felt emotionally abused by certain counselors, including a priest, to whom she turned for help. Having reflected on her experiences she constructed the following "Rules for Abusers of Power":

1. Never feel empathy for the one down. Assume they don't feel too bad, or that they'll get over it.
2. Never take the one down's problems seriously, certainly never to the point where you might advocate on her behalf.

---

[9] Cf. Alice Miller, *Breaking Down the Wall of Silence*, pp.97ff.

3. Correct her faults. That's what she needs. If she need punishing, hit her raw nerve, because she needs to be reformed.
4. Enlighten her and advise her from your superior perspective.
5. Remember the one down has nothing to offer. You may need to remind her how much you have done for her. The one down is ungrateful.
6. Never affirm the one down.
7. Never concede that she has a valid point to make.
8. Avoid listening to her or talking problems through, or you may be allowing her to manipulate you.
9. Never reply to her letters. Or if you do reply be non-committal.
10. If the one down complains that you're not being fair, it's her problem. You don't have to change. She shouldn't be angry.
11. Never apologize. Never admit a mistake.
12. Be assured you do love her, after all, you feel good towards her. Assure her of your prayers and unconditional love.

## IS THERE EVER A SOLUTION TO ABUSE?

Of course no-one would be naive enough to think that simply putting in place structures of accountability will "solve" the problem of power abuse in general or sexual abuse in particular. What we are talking about is shifting probabilities, from situations where it is more likely to occur and less likely to be detected, to a situation where if it does occur it can be detected and addressed before too much damage is done.

However, some are still naïve enough to suggest that structural change is useless unless you change the heart and minds of all those "in the system." This ignores the constitutive influence of social structures on human consciousness. Changes in structures do in fact change hearts and minds in the long term. Further, it is simply unjust to delay changes in structures until every individual in the system has been converted. This gives sin too much power and inevitably prolongs the suffering of the victims of abuse.

Further, structures are meant to be expressive of the meanings and values of the community and it is here that the deeper problems of power abuse lie. What is needed in the churches is a cultural shift away from a culture which sees ministry in terms of status, privilege and entitlement to one of service. As Jesus spoke of his own ministry:

> You know that among the Gentiles those whom they recognize as their rulers lord it over them, and their great ones are tyrants over them. But it is not so among you; but whoever wishes to be great among you must be your servant, and whoever wishes to be first among you must be slave of all. For the Son of Man came not to be served but to serve, and to give his life as a ransom for many. (Mark 10:42–45)

The abuse of power by those in ministry is antithetical to ministry as it is envisaged by Jesus. Until the Christian churches develop cultures and structures which minimize the possibilities of such abuse, they will not be following the example of Jesus.

## CONCLUSION: TO WHOM ARE WE ACCOUNTABLE?

Of course it would be naïve in the extreme to think that forms and structures of accountability to those "governed" would put an end to the abuse of power. That is not likely ever to occur, while ever we remain in a fallen, sinful world. What accountability does achieve is shift in the probability towards realizing a more just outcome for victims. It helps move us to a situation which more closely resembles the Kingdom which Jesus preached.

Indeed it is in the preaching, life and death of Jesus that we find the ultimate expression of accountability to victims. Jesus often draws to himself the symbolism of the Son of Man. This mysterious figure, found in the Book of Daniel (Daniel 7), represents a persecuted and victimized Israel. In Jesus' preaching it comes to represent his identification with all victims of the abuse of power, the poor, the naked, the imprisoned, the prostitutes, the lepers— "The Son of Man has nowhere to lay his head." In the apocalyptic discourse of Matthew 25 he uses this symbol to speak of his identification with the victims of history in the final judgment: "Whenever you do this to the least, you do it to me." On the cross Jesus' identification with the victims of history becomes complete, as he is sacrificed on the altar of a sinful humanity.

This is the accountability that Jesus speaks of in the Gospel. It is not the accountability to a harsh and exacting superior, waiting for us to step out of line, so that he can pounce—the archetypal abusive father. Rather it is an accountability to those below, to the victims, the abused, that Jesus speaks of. That the churches which speak in Jesus' name have not found adequate structures to express, within their own institutions, such an accountability (and this is certainly the experience of victims of sexual abuse and violence by church ministers), indicates how far the churches have to move to align themselves with the Gospel they preach.

# PART TWO

# CHAPTER SEVEN

# NO SAFE PLACE

*For most people a convent is the last place they would expect to find a victim of sexual abuse by a priest. Most would think that a priest would be the first to respect a woman's vows to the consecrated life. Yet this is not always the case. In the course of researching this book we came across a number of women in religious life who had been sexually exploited by priests. This is the story of one such woman.*

## 3 DECEMBER 1992

Jigsaw puzzles have always held a fascination for me. I see my life as a jigsaw with many small pieces whole in themselves, and yet only a small part of the more complete person that is me. When beginning work on a jigsaw, the first pieces to be looked out are the corner and edge pieces.

My hard working parents built a safe family home after the Second World War, into which I was born as one of the "baby boom" babies. They gave us a comfortable, no frills life-style which reflected their having survived a depression and the war.

Sunday Mass and Catholic schooling were important, but Dad wasn't a Catholic, so we didn't have much obvious religion in the home. My stated intention of becoming a sister took my parents by surprise, but my decision was accepted. I remember my father saying to me as I was about to get on the train to leave for the novitiate, "You can always come home you know."

We didn't show much physical affection, but moments like that one at the train station will always be remembered—I am a deeply-loved only daughter who is special to her parents. The pain of my story from that train station to now would leave them stunned and angry. I am too scared to tell them about it, but something deep in me wishes I could just be the little girl again, in that safe family, who could turn to her parents and cry, "Please protect me and fix this up."

The second stage of the jigsaw is that I always look for the easily identifiable parts, such as fences or buildings.

I entered the convent and had the normal mid-Vatican II novitiate, with all its pre-Vatican II restrictions: habits, traditions and practices and the confusion of impending change beginning to be felt. I was a "good young nun" who didn't rock the boat or ask awkward questions. I survived teacher training and went into school. Far too early I was appointed as principal—even though I did not want the position and asked not to be made a principal. The fact that I didn't even want to be a teacher was irrelevant.

I made my final profession. I fell in love with a student studying for the priesthood. This caused some problems. Because I had made my final vows, I was not free to fall in love. I didn't feel able to talk to anyone. This shouldn't be happening. I did what I thought was the right thing and told the guy to "get lost."

I was raped by a relative.

A sexuality came alive that I didn't know anything about. Masturbation became a dark and hidden problem, never to be spoken about.

I told nobody about the rape for four years, but in that time became alcohol dependent. Alcohol allowed me to escape from the hurt of memories. I learnt how to be a drinker and not get caught. A good priest helped me get over the guilt of the sins of drinking and self-indulgence and taught me how to drink socially—taught me not to be afraid of alcohol and myself. He was an important person for me.

A charismatic priest dug deeper and discovered the rape. In the process of "prayer," "healing" and whatever other euphemism you might like to think of, he emotionally and sexually abused me. The effects of this lasted for years.

Through the school scene another priest I met fell in love with me. I didn't know how to handle that. It was sort of flattering at first—but it turned bad. The relationship became sexual and in the end very abusive and manipulative. I had to end it, after nine or ten years, very bluntly and cruelly. I still carry guilt from it. Of late we have begun to cross paths in our work. I struggle with having to relate to him at a professional level. Memories of the past haunt me. I am unreasonably fearful of what he knows about me. I have to remind myself that I know just as much dirt about him. At present I sometimes feel as if I am on a tightrope at work, but a good boss and some counseling is getting me through the tense times.

My boundaries became very blurred. Several priests I made friends with seemed to do things to me and touch me in ways that I enjoyed but which caused conflicts of conscience. I had taken a vow of chastity.

Confession, guilt, shame and self-blame became a way of life. Of course it was usually stressed by the "confessor" that the woman is the stronger person, so I must take control of the situation. I look back over those times now with anger. It was a load of rubbish and should be discarded as such. Individual personal confession is no longer a part of my life. The whole sacramental stuff just seems to make the guilt even worse. I don't meet the God of compassion and forgiveness, only a man who heaps more guilt on me.

I attempted to talk to a provincial. She asked me if I wanted to leave the convent. She told me she could get the papers for me straight away and I could be on my way that day. I refused her offer and for years have just hung in from day to day.

I heard about Project Anna,[1] made some interstate phone calls from work where I had some privacy and found someone who listened, believed me, didn't blame me and gave me hope. I began that day to find the pieces of the jigsaw that said I wasn't crazy, this wasn't all my imagination and I wasn't to blame.

---

[1] Project Anna was a special project of the Centre Against Sexual Assault at the Royal Women's Hospital, Melbourne, Victoria, Australia, specializing in sexual abuse by church ministers.

The next part of the jigsaw are the pieces that are obviously identifiable, but not terribly big. It might be a rose on a bush, a tiny animal in a paddock or a bird in the air. All of these pieces are small details that usually give clues to the whole picture and stand alone, but in the beginning are not always obvious.

For me these pieces represent the important people in my life.

One is a novitiate friend who has always believed in me. She knows only a very little bit of my story and because of distance we don't see each other very often. She is faithful and loving. I don't know if she will ever realize just how important she is to me or if I will ever be able to tell her that.

My present provincial superior has recently listened to my story. She is the first and only one of my sisters to know so much about me. Her ongoing loving care over the last few months has given me hope that I do belong to my own congregation. I can't find the words yet to say just how important she is to me. I no longer feel so alone or so much of a hypocrite.

A sister, some years older than me, is important. She knows absolutely nothing of my story—only the good stuff and me as the presentable, successful church worker. She seeks out my friendship and I value that.

My parents are beginning to grow old now. They are very proud of their only daughter and their pride shows. My brother, his wife and family belong to the same mutual admiration society that I belong to. These are cornerstone people, but they appear as a thread throughout the puzzle. Their love is obvious.

There are other people, lay and ordained, women and men, who come and go as a part of my life for a period of time. They are a small part of the picture, but needed to complete the jigsaw. They have taught me when to trust and when not to trust—I have learnt some of the wisdom of the world from them. I am fortunate in being able to say, "these are my friends."

The final part of the jigsaw is the difficult stuff—the sky with a wisp of cloud, or a lake with subtle coloring. Often it becomes a matter of trying each piece in a painstaking way to see if it fits, before the jigsaw is finished. In some respects it all looks like mid-life journey stuff.

I do office work and often struggle to see it as ministry. The work suits my gifts and talents and I do a good job. I am beginning to believe that I would be missed now, not for the work I do, but for who I am. Maybe that says something about ministry. The pain, brokenness and guilt of my story gives me an ability to listen and accept people as they are now and not to make judgments. Other staff comment on my ability to listen and accept people without giving answers. It's all a bit of a mystery to me.

The spiritual part of my life could be considered to be a sham and failure. I am not at all sure what prayer is about any more. I go to Mass on Sundays because I don't feel free from the church laws yet. I haven't opened a breviary for about a year. Individual sacramental confession has been deliberately cut out of my life—it no longer makes any sense.

For me, individual confession just heaps more guilt on top of other guilt. I don't experience the peace and freedom that I believe should be a part of the sacrament. I struggle with all of this. I'm not too good yet at believing in my own experience and that I might just be right and others wrong.

So my prayer life and spirituality could be considered to be non-existent—but I don't believe it is. Externally there is not much to measure it by. If the above paragraphs were used as a measure of my prayer life I would end up with a minus score. I believe that God is bigger than all those external measures.

I sometimes write in a journal. I don't write every day, but when I do write it is a time of peace for me with a God who has always loved me and who loves me now as I am. I have made friends with some of the women of the New Testament. The woman taken in adultery and the woman at the well in Samaria are particular friends. I think those women understand what life is like for me. I often find myself having imaginary conversations with these two women. Maybe it's a form of prayer.

I often feel a desire to get some sort of revenge on the two priests who most abused me. I have a hate and a fear of them. I believe these Gospel women would understand my feelings. My feelings are not what I would have thought any good member of a religious order would ever have felt and I struggle to accept this in myself. The "turn the other cheek" stuff is nonsense. I know the two priests concerned are a "problem" for their bishops and for other women. I don't know how they are ever to be stopped from abusing women. I'm not sure that any bishop would believe me if I tried to tell him my story—and it would only be my word against the priest. I won't risk that.

Restless nights are spent with lots of reflection and trying to hear what God might be saying when all else around me is still. Constantly I am meeting a God of gentleness, quietness, patience and wonder.

I don't really know what community life is about any longer. I am still generally seen as the good sister who does the right thing—turns up to meetings, celebrations, and so on. But the people I live with don't know anything of my story and at this time I don't want to share it with them. It's lonely. I believe that sisters in the community would make judgments about what has happened to me. I fear that the appropriateness of my staying in religious life would be questioned. They will never know just how much I have questioned that myself.

I also haven't found my sisters to be good listeners. When I have tried to share some pain, such as a bad day at the office, the response is usually that I need to consider what is happening for the other person, see the other side of the story and that type of junk. They don't hear me saying "I am hurting."

While watching some recent television programs on rape with my sisters, the judgmental statements I heard and the general tone of the discussions left me stunned. I went silent and where possible left the room. It's as if they don't believe that any of this is ever real. The statements I was hearing from my sisters left me feeling like a slut. I felt angry, dirty, frightened and let down. So I usually live a life of pretence with my community—"everything is going fine". The sad thing, though, is that I seldom have the energy to bother sharing the good times.

I have a lot of anger towards community, past superiors and the system as a whole. Why weren't we told that we could fall in love? Why can't this be spoken of? Why can't they hear my cry for help? Why do I always have to make the first move? Will anyone ever not be afraid of my anger? Why is sexuality still such a big taboo?

Yet, in the middle of what seems like a community with no life for me, there is also that strange contradiction that says there is life present for me. A provincial who does care, an older sister who likes my company, a community I choose to live in that is happy, and a congregation that consciously respects the individuality and integrity of each person, are all important to me.

I celebrated my silver jubilee with the community last year. I was stunned at the number of sisters who made the effort to celebrate with me, who gave me gifts and wrote me wonderful things on cards. The cards have been bundled up. I find it too painful to read them yet—it's difficult to accept that they do care about me, do consider me a part of their community, do love me.

I'm not too sure what my vows mean today, but that's for the theologians to work out. I will just live as I believe God calls me to live today. In the midst of what so often looks like signs of the need to leave religious life, I have been aware of a God who is a relentless lover and will just not let go of me. My choosing to celebrate my silver jubilee was a very real choice: to say: "Yes, this is where I belong." It was a celebration of God's faithfulness, of God's continued call.

At the same time, not far below the surface, there is the guilt about what has happened in my life and that I haven't lived up to what a sister should be. I struggle not to condemn myself, or put "shoulds" on myself. I also struggle with my image of myself as a person who is a woman.

It sometimes doesn't take much to trigger the feeling of "dirtiness" that comes from the rape and prolonged sexual abuse by people I should have been able to trust—a careless remark by someone, a film clip on television, a headline in the paper—and I find myself heading for a long shower. This is not a serious difficulty, but the feeling that my body is dirty doesn't help much with my self-image as a woman.

I have allowed myself to become overweight. I am trying to address that problem now, but it's a struggle. I was going to Weight Watchers at one stage and felt good about myself while there, but a community member commented on the cost involved and I stopped going. I struggle to hold on to my own self-confidence and say it doesn't matter what others think. Because I present myself as very self-confident and professional, few people would realize just how sensitive I am to casual remarks. A careless remark from someone in the community can cut much more deeply than anyone ever is allowed to see.

One of my regrets is that as a community member, I feel I walk alone. I have found outside people who listen and have helped me believe again in myself. I would hope that no other sister would have had to go through a journey such as mine, but I believe I am not alone in this journey.

The final pieces of the jigsaw aren't in place yet. Life is over-shadowed by a fear that my story will become public knowledge and that people will want me to leave the congregation and my work. I fear that I will be blamed because things like those that have happened to me are "the woman's fault" and "what she asked for anyhow." It doesn't take much to trigger this fear, or shame or guilt—regardless of how unreal and unnecessary such feelings may be.

Learning to trust again, trust my own experience, trust that I won't be judged and rejected, trust that someone will see past the outbursts of anger, trust that they will know how to listen, is risky. Sometimes the risk is too great and I choose not to put the next piece of the jigsaw into place.

Writing this has been important to me. It helps me tell my story so that perhaps it will help someone else one day. Perhaps, too, it might help me reclaim some of my own integrity, self-worth and dignity. St Paul says somewhere that we are God's work of art. I certainly don't feel too much like that. God is either a rotten artist or the original picture has been damaged.

Some of the last pieces of the jigsaw have to do with self-nurturing, dignity, integrity, self-protection, being gentle with myself, discarding teaching well learnt for the initial formation days of a quarter of a century ago, and believing in myself. The pieces are getting closer to being put into their right place. One day, perhaps when least expected, they will all slip quietly into place and I will be able to marvel at the picture that has been made. Maybe one day I will be able to see the picture as God's work of art.

## 4 AUGUST 1993

It has been eight months since I first wrote about the jigsaw. Some significant friendships with men have changed. Sadly, these are much more acquaintances than friendships now. Some of my behavior has changed. I no longer touch people as easily as I have in the past. I am particularly aware of my own space and rights and when I will allow others to touch me. Sometimes I am awkward in greeting people and I sense that people are not sure how to greet me.

The illusions/dreams/hopes/beliefs, or whatever you may like to call them, that I once had about church and church people are gone. I now question people's motives, their basic goodness, their integrity. I question far more than I did in the past. Perhaps this is just coming to a maturity. Perhaps it is my way of facing reality and beginning to make sense of my story, my way of coming to life again. Perhaps also, it is my way of facing the reality that just because a person is an ordained minister does not mean he is automatically worthy of trust. Letting go of this belief is perhaps the most painful part of all. I thought all priests were good. I no longer believe that.

A couple of weeks after I wrote about the jigsaw in December 1992, another sister approached me with her story of abuse by a priest who had abused me. I was shocked and extremely angry. It was as though it was OK to hurt me, but not OK to hurt my friend. That anger was the catalyst that threw me into reality in a way I could not have anticipated.

The opportunity came to talk to a church official about a priest who had abused me. I kept stressing that it was my side of the story and that what had happened was over. I guess I had naïvely hoped that he would not continue to abuse other women. I know that the priest was confronted. He seems to have disappeared into oblivion and is soon to go away for some studies. I have told the church official that I do not believe study is the answer to the priest's problem, but I sense his superiors don't know what else to do with him.

For me there is relief that no longer am I keeping silent about what happened and no longer do I need to feel guilty with the fear that some other woman may be hurt because I kept silent. It seems that once the silence is broken—perhaps shattered is the more correct word—other stories of abuse within the church emerge.

Since December three other women have shared their stories of abuse by priests with me. Two of these women are getting along OK, but one is in need of specialist help. Her inability to take the steps to help herself, to get the counseling she needs is frightening. I can only listen to her and hope that one day she will find the key that will enable her to begin the journey of healing. As more stories emerge, as names of well-known and formerly respected priests become public, I continue to wonder where this will end.

There is a new anger in me, an anger that is enabling me to take charge of my life, to decide what is right for me, to take risks in letting people know my story, to continue moving from victim to survivor.

I struggle with what I believe were friendships with priests that didn't necessarily begin with counseling or pastoral relationships. I don't want to admit that there was a power relationship in these friendships. It's hard admitting that what I thought was friendship was in reality an abusive power relationship. And yet when I truly look at how all the friendships began, they were the result of spiritual direction or something similar. The reading I have done over the last year confirms that what happened to me was abuse from people in positions of power. In my head I believe this but at an emotional level I struggle to let go of the illusion that these men did care for me and were trying to help me, to let go of the idea that these men were friends.

Reading other abused women's stories has been frightening because so often another woman's story sounds like my own biography. Questions keep emerging: Is this what I am like? Is this what really happened to me? How did I let this happen? Why did this happen and when will it ever end? As other women now begin to share their stories with me, I see the pattern over and over again. The clouded thinking, the self-blame, the conspiracy of silence, the shame, the broken trust—all keep recurring. Will this ever end?

New friendships are being formed. I can't emphasize enough the importance of the support of people who know my story and who don't reject me once having read or heard it. It has now been shared with a number of people. The sharing has been remarkably freeing. From those I have trusted with it, I have met with nothing but acceptance. From those who have been abused themselves, there is an understanding that only comes from knowing the pain of abuse. From those who haven't been abused, I sense a bewilderment and perhaps the unspoken question, "How come someone as strong and respectable and independent as you got into such a mess?" It is becoming easy to tell from people's reaction to the story whether they have themselves been abused.

There is a pattern in moving from victim to survivor. I believe that there is a further stage, a stage I call "the coming of wisdom." It is the stage when patience and gentleness become a reality and the person who was once a victim now lives in peace—a peace based on reality and letting go of the past, with its pain and horror, while at the same time honoring that which must be respected. It is the stage where the wisdom of life's experiences truly brings forth new life, new expectations and new hope.

An anger often comes alive in me, but it is the anger that enables me to take appropriate action. Justice is important, but there is an acceptance also of what can be changed and what it is useless to spend energy fighting because it cannot be changed at this time. The jigsaw may be packed away for now, but that is appropriate. New calls are being heard, new people are coming into my life, new directions are being opened up, new patterns are being made. It's not always easy, yet there is an excitement and color about it that I like.

The abuse of the past should never have happened but in some strange way my life is all the richer now. Is this one of the paradoxes of life, that eventually out of evil, pain and loneliness, new life is born, holding all the promise of a different future and all the beauty of that which is tender and vulnerable in the present moment? Is this the stage of wisdom coming forth from deep within a woman and birthed through a passage of pain? For those who dare to face their nakedness upon the cross of life there does come a resurrection. Of this I am sure.

CHAPTER EIGHT

# A Sacred Betrayal

*Sexual abuse can involve not just the betrayal of the trust of ministry, but also the trust of friendship. In this story not only is the victim betrayed, but also her husband and the whole community to which they belonged.*

## The Calm Before the Storm

Something was nudging at my consciousness. It wasn't just burnout, although maybe that was part of it. I was in my thirties and had been leading a very full life raising a family, working part-time and involving myself in various social issues.

Working on these had been valid, but there'd been a drivenness about it. I could never seem to relax and trust in God. I also tended to feel bad about myself, was having recurring nightmares and was experiencing chronic lower back pain. There was no easy interiority. I was rather out of touch with my feelings and couldn't relate any more to that aspect of life people call the spiritual aspect.

I never much felt a sense of God's presence, not like I used to. All through my years growing up, until I was about twenty-three, I went to church services each week. I'd had what I experienced as a strong personal relationship with Jesus in those years. Now I wondered if it had really only been a shallow piety which evaporated when it was demystified. I prayed rarely now. God seemed distant and demanding. I felt I had to be as perfect as possible

123

before He would allow me a back seat in heaven. Still I saw myself as strong, as well provided for, in a position to act to save others. I didn't see myself particularly as a victim.

All this in the context of a marriage that had grown stronger as the years passed. It hadn't always been like that. Tom and I had always had a solid friendship, but in the early years there'd been something missing, the spark that makes the difference between friendship and love. At that time I was very distracted by a minister, the chaplain to our church youth group who we'd been very close to. This had ended up in a sexual involvement which had been very destructive at the time. I felt I'd thrown myself at him and got exactly what I deserved. But as the years passed I became increasingly angry at the minister in question, who I'll refer to as Pastor Joe. It began to bother me greatly that Pastor Joe was seen by people as someone who knew everything about love when in fact he knew very little.

I now knew love like I'd never known it before: in Tom's patient, attentive, sensitive, respectful caring about me. What I'd experienced with Pastor Joe contrasted so markedly I began to conclude that it mustn't have been love at all. I thought it was at the time. The whole youth group thought the world of Pastor Joe and he seemed to me at the time so pure and wise.

Not that I thought any of this had anything to do with my present malaise. That is not until a television program on the unethical nature of a psychiatrist's sexual involvement with a woman patient. I spent a whole night wide awake, in shock, crying, not thinking much, just realizing the priest had acted at least unethically! I had to check this out. I urgently made an appointment with someone whose judgment I respected immensely, a mentor I see now and again.

## THE NAMING

I told her the story and how I'd always understood it. She named what happened as "sexual abuse"! I was shocked. I wasn't at all convinced she was right. I argued with her saying I was an adult, it was I who would go to see him, I was infatuated. But she was unequivocal. This had been a relationship of most unequal power, with a professional whose responsibility it was to maintain sexual boundaries and it had been very damaging to me. I'd only ever thought of power as political, not as a factor in personal relationships.

I went home feeling incredibly liberated, if uncertain. I felt a great burden had been lifted. Perhaps I wasn't such a moral degenerate after all! I felt a whole lot better about myself. I wanted it to stop there, and leave the past behind except that now I saw it differently.

The only trouble was I couldn't sleep, or even eat. I was flooded with all sorts of feelings—anger at Pastor Joe (who at this stage I still loved) for what he had done, anxiety that the "sexual abuse" interpretation might be wrong, fear of how Tom would react if he found out. I felt a great flow of sheer unstoppable energy and a great sense of God's presence. A whole lot of pieces of a gigantic puzzle were coming together. The interpretation made sense of all the anger I'd felt toward Pastor Joe, the relationships I knew he'd had with other girls in the youth group, why I'd felt so miserable and out of control and confused when it was all happening, my loss of faith and why I never seemed to feel good about myself.

I kept running through the events in my head, testing the new interpretation. Was I also responsible for the sexual involvement? How did it all really happen?

## THE EVENTS AS I REMEMBER THEM

I met Pastor Joe when he was chaplain to our church youth group. I came from a deprived and abusive home background. I grew up unconfident, lonely and unhappy, my father was tyrannical. I would confide in Pastor Joe about relationship problems I was having.

I tried to leave home because it was unbearable. Pastor Joe was visiting at the place I was staying. He was in my room one night when he started to run his fingers around my bra and to try to kiss me on the mouth. I kept my mouth closed. I was simply confused and left the room.

A few nights later Pastor Joe invited me for a walk in the warm night air. It was a beautiful night, a bit of a breeze, a full moon. Walking with arms around each other, Pastor Joe was fun and romantic. I've never been so swept off my feet. Then he started trying to kiss me on the mouth again although I kept resisting, thinking this wasn't right, he was so much older than me. Eventually I let him kiss me the way he wanted. Still, I wasn't going to flirt with him, that was wrong, so I tended to avoid private times with him from then on.

Looking back now these incidents irreparably sexualized my relationship with Pastor Joe. From that time I didn't seem to be able to form normal feelings of attraction to guys my own age. Instead I was always attracted to this minister, but I didn't connect this with the incidents. In fact, I reproached myself for having a stupid schoolgirl crush. Pastor Joe did nothing to discourage my feelings. I saw him as very affectionate.

I tried to talk about my feelings towards Pastor Joe with a counselor, a mutual friend. Although normally very helpful, she advised me simply not to think about it. I tried to follow her advice, thinking maybe I was taking things too seriously.

At the same time Pastor Joe was conducting many church services and prayer groups for us, taking us on church camps, being a mentor and generally being our pastor. While I felt privileged to be around him I was also intimidated by him. I felt weak around him, like all the goodness was in him and none in me. I also found him confusing. He didn't show much empathy with uncomfortable feelings, which sometimes made him grossly insensitive. I didn't trust what my inner voice was saying. Instead I thought I shouldn't be so hypersensitive.

Soon after these events a lovely guy in the group proposed marriage to me. I believed Tom would be a wonderful husband and father, and even though certain feelings were missing for me, I thought they would develop with time. They didn't. I had a lot of trouble relating sexually to Tom. I developed a phobia for which I needed treatment.

I thought a child might bring happiness in my marriage with Tom. She did, but the attendant difficulties put even more strain on our relationship. I was in a stressful job and felt guilty about leaving the baby to be looked after by someone other than her mother. I wasn't coping well with life at all. I was in a fog. I confided in a friend that I thought my feelings for Pastor Joe were interfering in my being able to develop romantic feelings for Tom. She suggested I talk with Pastor Joe about them, so I approached him in the hope he could help me sort this problem out once and for all. I never dreamed he would react the way he did.

A week later he knew I was home alone and he called and asked if he could come over. I was delighted. Before I knew it we were in a bedroom and he was kissing me on the mouth again and unbuttoning his shirt. I said I thought this was wrong because I was married. He said it was good, we were just showing affection, we were friends, this is the way God gave people to show affection to each other. I found it very flattering. I believed him in a way, because I wanted to believe him and because his way of seeing things had always been definitive for me. I trusted him more than I trusted myself.

I went to see him again, by this time thoroughly infatuated. He kept telling me I was "beautiful," that what we were doing was so "simple" and "loving." Whenever we were together alone he told me repeatedly that what we were doing was simple. I was on a tremendous high when I was with him, and for a few days afterward, feeling privileged, like God himself was lavishing affection on me.

But between times I became depressed, longing only to see Pastor Joe again. The physical intimacy seemed to both heighten my felt need for his affection and my sensitivity to his approval or disapproval. It was only when we were physically intimate that I really felt his affection and approval. Otherwise, it was as though I didn't exist, and even when we did go for walks or just talked I found myself working hard to avoid his disapproval.

I would see him in a physically intimate way about every six to eight weeks. Each time he would take more and more initiatives and I began to think this was surely more than just showing affection. I genuinely wondered when one could begin to describe what we were doing as sexual, but when I tried to discuss this with Pastor Joe he said tersely that I should be able to work it out for myself. I began to be ambivalent and confused as well as depressed.

At this stage, in my eyes, Pastor Joe could do no wrong. I was beginning to think that what was happening was wrong, however, so I must be the sinful one. I felt less towards Tom than I'd ever felt. I wondered if I'd been terribly mistaken for both Tom's sake and mine to have entered into the marriage. Yet for me marriage was a commitment. I felt trapped, head over heels for someone who couldn't offer me a commitment, committed to someone for whom I could never seem to form proper feelings of attraction.

I couldn't seem to do a thing about my feelings. My life was out of my control. I began to feel intense love-hate toward Pastor Joe. I felt I needed him desperately, yet at the same time knew there was something extremely destructive going on. It was like an addiction, except there was someone I loved and admired telling me it was not only innocent but "love" and implicitly, therefore, good for me.

I found keeping the secret a terrible strain, because I'm normally very open with people and I couldn't lie. It was just such a contemptible problem. I was painfully conscious of how distant Pastor Joe was towards me when other people were around. The contrast between this and his intense "affection" in private would emotionally tear me apart. I became suicidally depressed for about five months. I cried every day, had trouble sleeping and planned ways of killing myself.

Tom thought Pastor Joe was helping me through this tough time I was having. He couldn't work out what was going on. No matter how hard he worked at our relationship, it seemed to be failing.

I tried a number of times to communicate to Pastor Joe how depressed I was generally. I cried sometimes and once I wrote to him, but to no avail. There was no way out. I was having so much trouble living with myself that I decided that if we did go as far as intercourse I would kill myself. So I resolved that I would never, ever allow him to take anything off below my waist.

This was repeatedly challenged one night. I was frightened, ashamed, confused and hurting. The next day I had to talk to him. I felt he didn't listen to how I was feeling. If anything, he seemed annoyed with me.

I went away a bit dazed, but slowly a lightness came over me. I noticed it was a beautiful sunny winter's day and I felt relieved.

I prayed to God, and in a moment snapped out of the depression. Looking back I now realize I split off from the feeling/child part of me. It was something I needed to do to survive, but at the time I understood it to be a religious conversion.

I saw him much less frequently after this, maybe five times over the next four years. I felt he expected it but to some extent I was still hooked. I became more and more determined to stop this somehow. When he was moved to a new parish I resolved that this was to be the end.

It was in these years that I seemed to lose the ability to pray. I lost myself in mountains of work. I became angry with the church, especially ministers because of their apathy about life and death issues. I thought a lot of what passed for religion was sentimental clap-trap.

## THE HEALING

I wasn't sleeping much at all. I wrote incessantly, including several letters to Pastor Joe. I was trying to contain the secret while finding an outlet to express all these feelings. It was as though the feeling/child part of me had been connected back with the rest of me, and sparks were flying. I was excited, feeling strong and liberated, vindicated, and as if God was embracing me. I experienced surprisingly strong feelings of sexual attraction to Tom.

At the same time I was infuriated with Pastor Joe. I was agitated about where all this would lead. My husband must never know. I felt so alone in this terrible secret world. The whole experience became so intense it felt as if my insides were being gouged out. I feared I was having a breakdown. I rang a telephone counseling agency but the counselor was quick to say I was to blame too, which only shook me more. As soon as I could, I went to see my mentor who referred me to a counselor.

After nine days of manic agitation and losing weight I felt I must tell Tom or break down completely. I was relieved he didn't blame me. Tom knew the significance of what I'd told him and was very protective towards me. He felt utterly betrayed by this person whom he had called friend for nineteen years, who had married us and christened our children.

Tom felt compelled to tell the church authorities about Pastor Joe's behavior. They knew this was important and that there were other women similarly affected. They planned to take Pastor Joe out of ministry and to insist he see a therapist. We wrote letters which he would be given to read. For a while they seemed to do the right thing. They paid for psychotherapy for me, something I now badly needed.

The therapist was very skilful in helping me really enter into and stay with my deepest feelings and work through them. I grieved for the father-figure who I thought had loved me and had only used me. I grieved for the lost years of my marriage, when I could have been so happy. I experienced again how affection-starved I was as a child and how badly abused emotionally, and how that left me vulnerable to any displays of apparent affection by parent-type figures. I found that I secretly despised that weak child in me that had left me so vulnerable and had caused me to feel so much pain. I learned to like her slowly. I came to accept my anger as OK, that I didn't have to turn it against myself. I raged, and cried, and raged.

Intermittently I would go into an anguished state of guilt. I felt terribly blameworthy and now I was hurting someone I still loved. At these times my image of Pastor Joe returned to one of him loving me tenderly but naïve in the expression of it. I still needed that love and would long to see him and be magically "reconciled." I would cry and sob and want to die.

Usually Tom was able to talk me out of these states, and I would return to feeling relatively OK and liberated. I promised him I would never actually do anything stupid. As the months went on these states would be brought on by the merest suggestion that I might be partly responsible for what happened, or by any pressure to be reconciled.

## Church Responses

The original youth group members had continued for years to meet together regularly. There was a commitment to nurture friendships we'd made in the context of many happy memories. We went away on camps together and became friends with other ministers. Tom and I felt some of these people had a right to know, because they saw Pastor Joe as a spiritual leader and we believed he would need their support in facing the truth.

Tom and I were writing to Pastor Joe. We told him in detail what we felt and thought and wanted an apology. The apology came. It was very emotional and eloquently phrased. He said he had loved me in what he saw as a fatherly way. He apologized for being partly responsible, for being naïve, insensitive and proud.

Tom and I saw this as the beginnings of repentance and wrote more letters. He wrote one more letter saying, among other things, he couldn't agree that what happened was sexual abuse. To me, if it wasn't "sexual abuse" then it must have been an "affair." That label had become unacceptable at a reasoning level and intolerable at a feeling level. I was frustrated.

Months had passed and we began to realize we were the only ones consistently trying to face Pastor Joe with what he had done. We felt we were being cast as the bad guys. The church authorities seemed to be losing interest. We felt isolated and betrayed, powerless and frustrated and in need of an advocate. We began to wonder if those responsible even saw this as a case of sexual abuse.

Friends in the community that had grown up around Pastor Joe were hurting too. They seemed to see what happened as a messy human situation in which two adults had gone off track. The pressure was on us to meet with Pastor Joe and be "reconciled." We knew such a meeting would bring back into play all the old destructive dynamics in the relationship and undo a lot of hard-won healing within me. We feared my inclinations to suicide.

It had only been a matter of months and there was already talk of Pastor Joe returning to full-time ministry. We protested but were assured by a church authority this was not so. Two weeks later Pastor Joe was back in his parish.

## SURVIVING THE SECOND ROUND OF ABUSE

We were shocked and outraged at Pastor Joe's return to ministry. Through letters we let the church officials know how we felt. I felt my truth had been completely discounted. I became unsure that what my inner voice was telling me was true. I felt shame, which led to guilt. It was as though a great shadow had fallen over everything and evil had the upper hand. I seemed to go from guilt into a defensive anger, from defensive anger back to guilt, and then back again to anger. Again, prayer became difficult. I kept searching my conscience, wondering if I was just being unrepentant. I became depressed.

I became very dependent on friends, especially Tom, to be assured that God still loved me. They were very patient with my emotional outpourings and generous with their time. I don't know how I would have coped without friends and a husband like that, because the healing process had become very complex. They became church for me. They held a special healing service for me and for Tom. Ministers and others I formerly related to as church were no longer church as I understood it.

Not all ministers. Tom received support all along from a minister he knew closely. There was another who was very supportive of me. For some reason I found him critical in my healing. His genuine humility and patient caring became very important to me. He demonstrated as well as talked about God's unconditional love.

But there was more trauma to come. Until now the local senior church authority had not involved himself in the issue. We'd heard he was a person of some integrity, so I wrote him a long letter stating as objectively as I could why Pastor Joe should see a good therapist and should not be continuing as a minister. I requested a proper apology from the church, as Pastor Joe seemed incapable of it. It would be so important for the healing of everyone, including Pastor Joe. I also asked if we could see him (the senior church authority) in person.

He did insist on Pastor Joe continuing in therapy. But no proper apology came and he couldn't "see the point" of meeting with us. I couldn't believe it. I kept turning over and over in my mind: What could he be thinking? But I would never know what the blockage was because he did not enter into any meaningful dialogue. I felt punished and worried that I deserved it. He was now feeding the guilt in me. Sometimes I cried and cried. Sometimes I raged. Again, mostly at night.

Tom and I began to pull in different directions. Tom wanted to forget the whole church. Most of our attempts to communicate with them had elicited no support and sometimes thinly veiled accusations. All their talk about compassion, love and justice over the years took on a deathly hollow ring. I felt there must be a misunderstanding. I didn't want to face the reality that was staring at me: that the church which had been my spiritual home was in fact an unsafe place for me and there was no way of making it safer in the short term.

Life did go on. The kids both needed us and brought us a lot of joy in what was otherwise an awful mess. My own healing was still very incomplete, especially because guilt was still an issue.

## The Defeat of the Guilt Monster

In the middle of all this I stopped working. I had to delve into what caused me to be so easily unnerved by any suggestion that I was partly responsible. Why could I not have confidence in my own truth?

More formidable than any outside opposition was the guilt that gnawed away at me on the inside, in spite of all the understanding I had gained. A breakthrough came when I realized God had forgiven me but somehow I wasn't forgiving myself. But the guilt issue remained unresolved.

I had switched from the therapist to a counselor. It was less expensive for one thing. She'd been generally challenging, rather than supportive, but in the fourth session she actually suggested I might be feeling guilty because it was appropriate that I feel guilty! I was an adult after all and Pastor Joe hadn't used force. Outwardly I went into defense. Inwardly I was badly shaken and unsure.

Four days later someone else made the same suggestion, another professional. I was cast headlong into the most tormented state ever. *None* of it would have happened if I'd had a fair measure of control! I felt Pastor Joe had used my trust and vulnerability and his power as a pastor to hook me in and keep me hooked! People were seeing me as I am *now*, stronger and more knowing ... very different from who I was then.

It was no use! It was as though there was a monster in me that had just been fed. It had two heads, guilt and shame. I'd been trying to starve it in the last year, so now any food, the merest morsel, gave it just enough energy to roar in violent protest. I felt every cubic inch of me was consumed with guilt, as though I were in hell already. I wished I had never been born. I wanted desperately to die, but I couldn't ... I had three kids to look after. I wanted the magic of forgiveness, but that would mean admitting responsibility, and that was unthinkable. There was no way out.

Another breakthrough came when I realized where some of this guilt was coming from. My mother had taught me attitudes about sexuality I'd never consciously rejected. I was loath to reject anything at all about my mother. I'd always idealized her. In various subtle ways she taught me that sexual sins are the most damnable of all, that it was up to me as the girl to keep myself chaste, that I should be careful not to be seductive. Not: be careful, men can take advantage of you. I took the opportunity to consciously dump that baggage. Without intending to, Pastor Joe had superimposed the implicit message, "I love you for your sexual availability" on my mother's message, "The girl is responsible for avoiding immoral sexual involvements."

But the torment returned a week later, more ferociously than ever. I went for a bushwalk, something I always found to be soothing. But not this time. I cried uncontrollably because I was sure I was going to hell no matter what. I'd been adulterous towards my beautiful husband. I was the lowest of low-life. I couldn't go on living this way. Perhaps I was experiencing hell because that's what I deserved for all my unrepentance. I felt cut off from God. I stood at the top of a cliff losing my resolve not to suicide. It frightened me to be losing that resolve. Somehow I turned around and made my way home.

Thank God for good friends. Slowly at the core of my being I saw that this "God" who I felt to be punishing me wasn't God at all. It was a false god, a guilt monster that had been planted in me not only by my father ... but my mother ... and the church, to extract obedience. Pastor Joe had simply given it plenty to grow big and mean on. A peace settled over me, because the guilt monster was substantially defeated.

## DIALOGUE WITH THE SENIOR CHURCH OFFICIAL

I sought and obtained three professional opinions on the nature of Pastor Joe's sexual relationship with me, from a psychiatrist, a sexual assault counselor and my former therapist. They all named it as sexual abuse. Finally I felt strong enough to take another rejection and we sent the reports and another letter to the senior church official.

He agreed to meet with us. But it had been over eight months since we originally requested it. Our inability to trust him, given all that had transpired, made quality communication virtually impossible. He apologized for adding to our suffering, and listened ... but he didn't understand. He agreed to begin paying again for further therapy, but failed to make any of the tough decisions needed to effect justice. His official apology for the abuse was, "I regret what happened." He later told someone else he believed Pastor Joe had repented. I think now he didn't understand the language of the heart. It's a language ministers speak and one is deceived into thinking they understand it, but they don't.

Tom and I do believe in the justice of God, and that's what gives us hope now.

## NOW

It's now been two years since the naming. I still struggle with despair and guilt at times in therapy and when I try to pray, but the feelings are not nearly so intense. I'm learning to nurture the inner child that can feel so bad. And I'm learning to trust the real God.

What's left to sort out is my shattered relationship with the church. I feel unsafe in the church, therefore spiritually homeless. My faith is more important to me than anything and I want to give the faith to my children, and also I need to belong. But I cannot stomach the way the clerical class has the power and the way they use it to serve their own interests, all while talking to us about love and prayer and God. I know many people on the edges of the church who feel the same way. Perhaps these can be some kind of church for me now.

I've learned a lot. About what it means to be fully alive. I've discovered who my true friends are, what true friendship is and therefore more of who God really is. I've reluctantly recognized the church's capacity for evil as well as good. I've learned about the role of power in relationships and what it's like for people when power is abused. I hope this is making me a better parent.

Best of all, a new me is emerging out of the mess. My friends comment positively on the change. I understand better now both my fragility/need of love and the power I have within to hold to my own truth. I only hope that what I've learned can be used to help other people.

CHAPTER NINE

# A HISTORY OF INDIVIDUAL
## VULNERABILITY

*Perhaps none are as vulnerable to exploitation as those who are placed in the care of church institutions because of difficult or tragic family circumstances. These are people most in need of care and protection, yet often what they find is abuse. Here is the story of one man who has struggled with his own history of sexual abuse at the hands of church ministers.*

I am a forty-six-year-old bachelor who is firmly attached to the Catholic church. Strangely, the religious faith I questioned, doubted and resisted for two decades now provides a strong, if not unshakeable, foundation and purpose for my living, while the consolations of prayer and spiritual experiences over the years have given me a sense of contentment and peace which I hope, God willing, always to retain. I recognize that my Catholic beliefs and sensibilities permeate the whole of my life and most define who and what I am. Nothing is more important to me than the Catholic church.

Yet it was priests and religious brothers within the church who abused me sexually and took advantage of my vulnerability as a child and my earnest searching as an adult. Only within the church have adult men sexually touched my body without my permission. Those priests and religious brothers are exploiters and opportunists; they have the problems. I am not—and never was—the eternal victim handing out cards saying "I'm yours for the taking."

My mother became ill when I was two-and-a-half years of age, and my brother and I were sent to St Michael's orphanage and our

137

two sisters were cared for by a grandmother. At eleven years of age, I followed my brother to a Catholic boys' home which was staffed by religious brothers. When I was twelve years of age I slept in a dormitory supervised by Brother X. I remember two occasions when I was in the recreation room next to the dormitory, along with Brother X and a number of other boys. It was after the rosary period and all of the boys were dressed in pajamas. Brother X picked me up in his arms and pressed me tightly against his torso and stomach and then rubbed his whiskered chin against my face. On both occasions I pulled away. Brother X asked something like, "What's wrong?" I recall replying, "Stop it. I don't like it." He tried to make a joke of it, as if I was somehow at fault by not joining in what he made out was a game. He continued to play his game with other boys. One night he lifted up a boy, and the boy kicked him in the shins quite hard and shouted "Get away." Brother X became very angry and threatened to cane him. It seemed to me then that the boy was being disrespectful towards the brother.

Brother X initiated his game, presumably out of his own desire for touch and affection. Although most of the boys did not object to being involved, he included in it boys who were unwilling. When he was questioned about his behavior many years later, he acknowledged he did touch boys in his little game, but he claimed he was giving affection to those who needed it. My present-day fear is that, having disregarded the boundaries of personal autonomy in the way described, Brother X went on to more serious forms of inappropriate behavior, though he apparently denies that he did so.

I was still at the same Catholic boys' home four years later. I didn't like being there and, in common with many of the boys, I put up with the physical and emotional abuse as an unchangeable fact. I guess we were highly institutionalized. It was at this time that I had the misfortune of being in the dormitory of a religious brother who was a persistent sexual offender. Over a six-month period in my final year at the boys' home, he systematically molested me. I never told anyone when it was happening. The assaults occurred at night, and against my will. I was extremely naïve and had absolutely no experience of anything sexual. Though fifteen years of age I had never stimulated my own genitals and I had never touched another person's body in a sexual way, nor had anyone touched mine sexually. Apart from the first assault, the pattern of abuse was the same. It took place where I slept and despite my childish methods of evasion (for example, wrapping myself tightly in the blankets) and my telling him, "Stop. Go away." During the assaults I dissociated from my body and shut off my feelings. My mind stayed alert, but I could not understand why he was doing what he did. I linked the assaults to the brother's unfair punishments, as if they were a new extension of them; yet I knew I had done nothing wrong to warrant punishment. Equally I knew that I did not want the brother so near me physically, let alone have him touch me. I successfully repressed the trauma of the abusive episodes for thirty years. A television program on sexual abuse within Christian churches was the trigger to my telling a counselor, and that in turn led to my informing the church and civil authorities. The brother pleaded guilty to three counts of indecent assault and he was convicted and sentenced by the District Court.

After leaving the boys' home, I worked in a bank for three years, and then returned to high school to complete my studies. At that school I was indecently assaulted by a Catholic priest when I was eighteen years of age. I was in a group of senior students waiting to be served at the canteen. There was usually a lot of milling around and Father Y was ostensibly there to control the crowd. On two afternoons Father Y touched me on the buttocks and on the inside of my upper thigh. When this occurred, I either moved or pushed his hand away. The first time I did not say anything, but the second time I said, "Cut it out!" or something to that effect. Father Y gave one of his silly smiles and said something like, "But it doesn't hurt." I replied along the lines that I did not want him touching me anywhere. Father Y often pinched, rubbed, rested his hand on and otherwise touched students, but whether he ever went any further than that I cannot say. The senior students used to snigger at Father Y's behavior and speak about him disparagingly. I decided to inform the school's principal about Father Y's immodest activities and told him what had happened to me, what I had seen, and what other students were saying. He heard me in silence and I felt very foolish and awkward. At the time I presumed that the principal would speak to Father Y, in order to ensure that he stopped his activities. I now believe that he most likely did nothing.

There are another four priests who acted inappropriately towards me, all in my adult life. In the early 1970s I was a university student travelling by overnight train to an anti-war conference. I was sharing a two-bunk compartment with a Catholic priest, Father V. The two of us chatted about conference business for three hours in the dining car and in the compartment before deciding that it was time to retire for the night. I kept on my clothes, climbed to the top bunk and was soon drifting off to sleep. I was woken by Father V, who had put on a night-light and called out, "Look at this." I peered down, and there he was naked and lying on his stomach. I sort of grunted, "What?" And he said, "Isn't my rear end nice?" I replied, "I wouldn't know." He said, "Well, look at it." I responded that I had no interest in looking at it. His final comment was, "Many of my friends say I have a nice rear end". I said nothing, and he went quiet. With the train's gentle rocking and the silence, I managed to get to sleep. Father V never again referred to any part of his anatomy and I must say he at no time touched me.

The years went by and I followed various careers, changing jobs and cities frequently. My next encounter with a sexually dysfunctional Catholic minister occurred when I was thirty years of age. I had been going through a crisis of faith for more than a decade. Passing a church one afternoon after work, I decided to go to confession to a priest not known to me. I began by explaining to the priest that I had not been to the sacrament of penance for a while and that I had not been following the church's teaching on sexual morality, specifically in relation to sexual acts between consenting single adults. I told him that, although I did not consider such acts to be intrinsically wrong, out of respect for the magisterium I had ceased regular attendance at the sacraments, going to communion only when I was in what the church officially deemed to be "a state of grace." The priest questioned me about the nature of the sexual acts and determined that I was not in a relationship. He then described how he had a friend with whom he went to the gym, dinner and—he implied—

elsewhere. Father Z next talked about how the gym was a good place to meet men, especially in the sauna. He asked me if I would go with him to the gym. I declined politely. He next asked me to go out to dinner with him, where we could "get to know one another and become friends". I again declined, saying that I was too busy to make new friends. Finally, he asked if I would "have a coffee" with him, as he was just about to finish for the evening. I said I would not. It was clear to me at the time that Father Z was telling me he was homosexually inclined and had a special male friend, and that he was keen to see me outside the confessional and to befriend me. I drew the conclusion then, as I do now, that he was implying he was sexually active and that we could be so together.

I left the confessional shaking my head and doubting that I had really been propositioned. It never occurred to me to complain at the time, mainly because I was so preoccupied with resolving my dilemmas of faith and religious practice. I went to confession intent on receiving a priest's counsel regarding those dilemmas, most particularly on how I might be able to reconcile my sexual activity, which I conscientiously believed not to be sinful, with regular reception of the Eucharist. Father Z instigated the discussion about homosexual friendships and he displayed sexual opportunism with absolutely no encouragement from me. It was a shameless misuse of the confession. His misconduct did not lead me away from the church, but repeated with others of less robust faith it could well have led them to reject the church. I finally informed the Catholic authorities a few months after I discovered the adverse effects of the religious brother's systematic sexual abuse on me at the boys' home.

The remaining encounters were with priests I knew quite well, one of whom I considered a friend. I had been invited by Father J to dinner at his presbytery. I accepted, assuming there would be other guests. There weren't and it was the housekeeper's night off. Father J had prepared an impressive meal and provided good wine and soft lights for the two of us. I drank sparingly, as I had to drive home. We discussed various topical issues, including a church project we were jointly working on. Father J suggested we have after-dinner coffee in another room, and I agreed. I thought it a bit odd that he sat alongside me on a two-seater lounge, as there were plenty of other seats available. I was surprised when he put his arm around my shoulder, but I did not object as I thought it might hurt his feelings and be interpreted as an over-reaction on my part. He commented on his need for friends who could share with him on an intimate level. I was indirect and as polite as possible in what I said in reply. As well as putting his arm across my shoulder, he also moved his leg against mine where we sat. He talked more about his intimacy needs, while I hankered for a suitable break in the discussion so that I could leave. The break came from an unexpected source. The housekeeper had returned early and her heavy footsteps in the hall could be heard. She entered the room without knocking, saying she thought someone had left the lights on by mistake. Before she opened the door, Father J had rapidly withdrawn his hand and shifted to another chair. I left soon after.

The other episode took place with a priest in my own home. Father Q had called by unexpectedly and wanted to know how I was feeling. I explained my anguish at the institutional church's uncaring response to my revelations of sexual abuse at the boys' home. Father Q was initially sympathetic but went on to comment that perhaps I needed to forgive the perpetrator and get on with my life. I told him that his remarks were unhelpful, and that I needed to have my hurt accepted for what it was. He had been sitting close to me up to this point, and I did not feel in any way uncomfortable. He put his arm around my shoulder and said I needed affection and asked if was I getting it. I replied equivocally, not to encourage him but because that was how I saw the issue. He put his hand on the inside of my thigh, and I moved his hand back onto his own leg. He then put his hand on my genitals and said a massage would relax me. At this, I said forcibly, "What are you doing?" He repeated his massage line and I told him that I most certainly did not need that. Out of politeness I omitted saying that I did not need it from him. Before leaving that day Father Q wanted to be hugged, and I agreed to that.

I am not the eternal victim, as I said earlier. Only within the church have I been subjected to sexual abuse and unwanted sexual touching and proposals by adult males. I am still coming to terms with the most serious of the sexual assaults, but my healing is well under way and my personal wholeness is being restored. I am once again happy, and I look forward to living an integrated life which is free of the insidious effects of the worst sexual assaults. Despite this progress, I am not yet able to comprehend why the Catholic church harbors such dysfunctional ministers. For many people the city is an unsafe place. For people like myself the church has been even more unsafe. But where can I go? I am a cradle Catholic and I will most surely die a Catholic. However imperfectly, I have sought to serve God and others in and through the church in the past, and I trust I will continue doing so for years to come. I know the answer to my own question: There is nowhere for me to go, not when I am already in the church I love.

# CHAPTER TEN

# NOT ONLY MEN ABUSE

*Throughout this book we have spoken of ministers as "he." In this account it becomes clear that it is not only men in ministry who are capable of sexual abuse. In the Catholic tradition women in religious life have exercised a real ministry in the life of their communities and in other churches women have been welcomed into ordained ministry. In these positions of power they too are capable of abusing the trust of those in their care.*

As one of many invisible spectators in a theatre, I was meant to be a non-partial witness to the unfurling of a deliberate act of revenge by a woman against her rapist. She was awesome in her self-possession. He was as pathetic in his middle-age maleness as he was equally sinister some fifteen years earlier in his zealous adherence to patriotic correctness. The darkness of the auditorium jerked me out of the play's Chilean setting into my own subterranean memory of the act of indecent assault by a nun that fuelled my propulsion for retaliation of a like kind. Unlike the female persona of this play's name, "Death and the Maiden," I would never be able to live out my revenge except as played out in the innumerable screenings of my subconscious. In my real world I could never allow myself to come face-to-face with my "spiritual assassin." I am balanced enough to never grant myself permission to point a gun directly at her face, unlike this heroine.

Instead, I am invaded, though not by conscious invitation, with images of our numinous reunion in some imaginary courtroom in future time—where I rush out of my courtroom stand and walk with accelerating purpose towards my perpetrator. Within a breath of a pause, I have pulled out a knife from inside my skirt pocket and plunged it into her, again and again and once more. I do it with a conscious focus and without remorse.

Regaining my posture back in the real world, I push it away through shame of ownership to its ethereal lodging, till our next undisclosed appointment. That could be another time within the same day, or tomorrow or whenever it spies a convenient opportunity for occupation. The scenario never changes in hue or kind—never. It has been protected in a thick wall of silence, the main agent being a mutual collusion between my shame and the ignominy of such an act. For this is one dimension of the inheritance from my one-off assault which I have endured for twenty-seven years.

The act took place when I was a seventeen-year-old school girl attending a convent school in the inner west of Sydney. It was towards the end of November, 1966 and school activities were beginning to wind down in anticipation of summer holidays and the transition into the Wyndham Scheme[1] which was to come into effect the following year. This meant that fifth form students like myself had to transfer to other schools which catered for the new syllabus. As a treat one afternoon the nuns had arranged a screening, in our dingy school hall, of Oscar Wilde's "The Importance of Being Earnest"—a play in which I and other students who laid a claim to dramatic potential, had performed.

I was summoned away from the regimented column of girls by one of the nuns, who said I was to go straight away to see the Principal in her office where she was expecting me. Grudgingly I obeyed, hoping that whatever it was all about would be over in a matter of minutes and I could stake my place to a good viewing position downstairs. I also recall being rather preoccupied with the condition of my summer school uniform as the nuns were fiercely protective of their image of unsullied competence being relayed to the outside world by their well-trained ladies.

---

[1] The Wyndham Scheme involved a major restructuring of high school education in NSW, adding an extra year to high school studies.

I shall spare you description of the Principal nun's physical characteristics, only to say she was of ample frame in terms of some of the characters from the early 1950's carry-on comedies that featured men in drag—Lionel Jeffries would be an appropriate example. But I flatter her with a sense of humor—her inward laughter, betrayed by the curled corners of her tight mouth, trailed into a smirk that emanated through the debasing and humiliation of one of our miserable number.

I faced the black and white habit in a somewhat bemused state. I had never been summoned to the Principal's office before—this was something of an initiation for me. She proceeded to inform me in her best no-nonsense, formal demeanor as befitted her rank, that I was to be expelled immediately and was ordered to remain upstairs in the classroom vicinity until the film had ended and the rest of the girls had gone home. When I asked her the nature of the transgression she refused to discuss the matter with me. If I wanted further clarification she recommended I discuss the matter with my head teacher, Sister A, after school.

During the two and a half hours spent within the confines of a toilet cubicle or the verandah outside the classroom, I dredged my memory for traces of evidence that would warrant this most serious of penalties. I must have done something horrendous or utterly immoral somewhere along the line. Only petty minor irritants surfaced. Then it must have been something I said. The school's library—that treasured room for our seclusion and open discourse—suddenly came to mind in a murky and tainted light as the outline of an intercom positioned high in a corner impressed itself into my visual recollection.

I again attempted to meticulously retrace my movements and company of that and the previous day, in particular my "free period" which my best friends and I normally spent, as ordered, within its sparsely shelved walls. My turbulent recollection of that half hour only left me with vague memories of our conversation, whose general themes centered that day around too much Catholic doctrine and the poor academic training standards of the majority of the nuns, with the exception of our competent science teacher and our lay teachers. I could only vaguely recall a conversation about some aspects of the crucifixion and resurrection which were strongly testing my tentative faith, not to mention my Catholic practice at the time. Or worse still, I may have speculated on the suppressed impulses of the nuns' sexuality.

Whatever the nature of my sin, I was overwhelmed with shame for my parents and self-disgust for having failed their emotional and financial investment in me, their firstborn and, to their Depression and war-ravaged Eastern European sensibilities, doubly privileged with an Australian *and* Catholic education. My father especially denied himself even a decent pair of leather sandals (always plastic) so that my brother and I could have that Catholic tutelage, for the best of Catholic doctrine came directly from him by example. He was an ex-religious—a former Sacred Heart brother—who had known selflessness not only as an attribute of his devoted faith but through being the youngest of eight children in rural Czechoslovakia. In his mid-twenties, after leaving a Viennese seminary, he became a missionary in the New Guinea highlands for twelve years which took in the Second World War and the Japanese atrocities, leaving him weakened with the after-effects of malaria and shell-shock for the remainder of his life. He had been ill with a heart condition for the last four years, especially the year in which my assault took place.

It was about 4:30pm in the afternoon when I entered our classroom and approached Sister A. She was writing on the blackboard and had her back to me. By a minute head movement she saw me enter and her tall bearing resumed its position, intent on breaking me into her space. I spoke first and in tears apologized for any wrongdoing I might have done and begged to know the nature of my transgression. Avoiding my eyes she said curtly, "Surely you know," and refused to discuss it any further. Insisting I had no idea was not going to elicit any further light on the subject. She held her rigid ground in silence.

Eyes averted she moved towards her desk in the middle of the raised platform and commenced to inform me that in her opinion there would be no point in my continuing with my education as I would never make it to university nor successfully complete any academic course. And further, in her opinion, I could never successfully complete my high school education. To support her judgment she thought I should know that she had read the results of my IQ tests conducted the year before and the results showed that my mental ability was below average, since my score, she said, was below 95. I felt decimated.

The next thing I knew, she had moved close to me and tightly pulled me in towards her. Gathering me in her arms, she began to kiss me forcefully, sliding her tongue deep inside my mouth. It lasted for about ten seconds till I could jerk free from one of her hands that had started to stroke my breast.

In a faltering, barely audible voice, I said I had to go home and quickly walked out of that room. I crossed the convent grounds and passed the tennis courts in a numb daze and tried to compose myself when I noticed that about half of our small class of fourteen had been waiting for me, including some of my best detractors from the Sports/Science camp. They were intrigued and genuinely concerned as to what happened as this detention had not occurred to any of my group before. I told them nothing of my meeting with Sister A, not even my best friends. All I was capable of divulging was that I was threatened with expulsion and because there were only two or three weeks remaining till the end of the school year, and because of my desperate apologies, they would let me stay on to see out the school year.

When I got home I kept to my room and never told my parents what had passed. My next vivid recollection of Sister A was two weeks later, at my father's funeral, when both she and the Principal attended as official representatives of the school and the church. It was the usual practice on these occasions for pupils of the school to attend the Requiem Mass, either to sing or to perform a guard of honor outside the church for the funeral cortège. None of this was done for my father. Only my best school friends attended. The others were never told of my father's death as it was now school holidays and they would all be attending new schools in the next year.

There is too much to say of the consequences for myself of this assault, most of which I will not touch on here. However I will briefly outline three. The most significant is my estimation of myself, of my worth, and of how I am scrutinised and assessed by others. I have been engaged in conscious and subconscious warfare ever since with the evil of appallingly low self-esteem, which oscillates according to the quality of nurturing and positive affirmations that I am at times too frightened to receive. I challenged myself to study and complete high school as a mature student—being one of 120 successful students out of 1200 who were offered places at Sydney University—managing the workload of study and working full-time every year but one. I finally graduated with respectable results. Nevertheless I still cannot stop believing, in part or in whole—this I cannot judge—her conclusion from IQ results that I am "below average."

Secondly, I have a palpable fear of a type of dominating, assertive, very confident female intellectual kind (especially the tall).

Finally, there is the issue of forgiveness. Am I able or do I want to? According to one of the nuns from Sister A's order, she cannot remember the incident and her abuse. Without some acknowledgment of time and place at the very least, she is not offering any room for negotiation on this critical issue. I waiver and submit half-heartedly towards forgiveness, knowing there is no choice left for me except an imploding, destructive hatred. So I try again to get on with my life.

But it is not honest, real or whole. True forgiveness cannot be granted till my suffering has been owned by her as real. Until she can find the courage to own up to the full dimension of her humanity and admit her transgressions, our mutual healing and enlightenment can never be complete.

# CHAPTER ELEVEN

# NOT JUST THE VICTIM

*Being sexually abused by a church minister is horrific, but being the parent of an abused person is also devastating. A church minister, whom you have welcomed into your home, has taken advantage of your generosity to abuse your child. In this story a mother of an abused person tells her story of betrayal, not just by the perpetrator but by a church community which failed to protect her son and eventually forced her out by its efforts to protect the perpetrator.*

## A MOTHER'S STORY

I was enjoying a read in bed when my son John arrived home and came into my room to tell me something. He blurted it out, said he couldn't stay and left. The next day he rang to see if I was alright. His news had left me knowing I would never be the same again. It was the end of one way of life and the beginning of a new one.

There is never a good time to tell your mother that the youth minister she had invited into her home had sexually abused you for years. My thought that night went back to our first meeting with him at church as the new youth minister. It had taken the church some time to find him. Right age, right background and reputation, did things the boys enjoyed and had time to be a friend because he wasn't married. He said he was like his dad and would marry later on. It was important he find the right person, given he was in Christian work. He carried a big Bible under his arm and enjoyed singing and music.

One night he talked to my husband and me. Our son was one of the boys at church he believed had potential for leadership and he wanted to train the group. This meant having a closer friendship and spending more time with them. There would be Bible studies, time to talk and do "boys' things" as he took the role of friend and guide through their adolescent period. We talked about his role as youth minister, and the need to give all the young people time. He assured us he had thought about these issues, that our son would always be cared for, and we agreed to his proposal.

He became a regular visitor to our home and joined us for meals and birthdays. I couldn't count the number of meals I gave him over those years. Our family always ate together in the evening so he joined in our discussions. I know we talked about child protection and sexual abuse because of my work with children. It's a wonder he didn't choke on his food, he always said the right things and gave away nothing to cause alarm. We went on holidays and he brought some of the young people from church for weekends. He did this with other families and took John. John never went away on his own. When my mother-in-law was dying I left my youngest son with him while my husband and I went to the hospital to be with her. I trusted him completely.

I often talked to him about my sons, their problems and how they were getting on. We talked about his work at church and with other organizations. He seemed to be confident, sure of himself, and open about his own life. I was pleased for him when he became engaged, pleased that he would have someone to care for him. He often talked about the Christian life and living that life. I always supported him and prayed his ministry with young people would lead them to a faith and trust in Jesus Christ which would make a difference in their lives. I have spent much time thinking about him these past years and how much effort he must have put into maintaining his youth minister appearance. It must have been a deliberate effort, sustained over a long period of time.

Some people don't believe parents could not know what was happening to their child. I believe it could happen to any child within the church as easily as it happened to John. The church introduces a youth minister to the congregation as part of the ministerial team. He is employed by the leaders of the church, presented as a Christian leader of integrity, with Christian beliefs, values and personal standards, a person you can trust. His role is to lead and guide your children as they grow and mature spiritually and socially. The youth minister holds a position of trust, power, authority and respect within the church community and the wider field of the whole denomination. His role within the Christian world is very extensive. He is usually well known by a large group of people.

Why should parents be suspicious of a youth minister? Why should they doubt what he said? Who would think he had a secret life? Christian parents do not expect the youth minister to be on the look out for young boys. They don't expect him to be a pedophile looking for boys in a place where he is trusted. Criticize me for making a mistake in trusting the youth minister if you want, but other people are probably doing the thing I did and trusting a youth minister with their child. I acted not out of ignorance or lack of care for my son, but out of trust, trust that the youth minister was who he said he was—a person who would encourage and foster the spiritual growth of young people within the church family.

The day after John told me I went to work—it was all done automatically. I sat in the car park and cried. I spent my professional life caring for children and my own son had been sexually abused. I felt I must somehow be responsible and that I had no right to be doing my job, I had no professional credibility any more. As a mother I was devastated, I felt as if I had been chewed up and spat out. It has taken me a long time to regain enough confidence in myself to be a mother to my sons again. I can't write about how I felt, the hurt is still too deep. I can only say the anger and pain at times have been overwhelming. My health and faith have been affected, relationships broken, trust betrayed and gone and I am not the person I used to be.

John's father worked in the Boys' Club at church for many years, caring for other people's sons and he loved his son dearly. He was devastated by the news, overwhelmed with grief and broken in spirit. Several weeks later he was diagnosed as having a serious illness. I asked God not to let him die while he had so much pain in his spirit. He needed healing from his hurt and pain. God healed his spirit in a miraculous way but he died within several months. He didn't want to leave his family and there could not have been a worse time for him to die. I needed him, John needed him, our family needed him. My husband had two regrets about his life, one was that he had taken his family to that church, the other was that he had invited the youth minister into his home. Before he died, he knew in his spirit that we would be alone and few from church would stand by us. He said the leaders would act to protect the church and those who had known about the abuse before we did. That knowledge made it more difficult for him to leave us.

The youth minister wasn't pressured. He admitted to several people what he had done and that he viewed my son as his victim. There was no fight with him for the truth. Here was a person who had been to counseling, who knew who he was before coming to our church, who knew youth ministry would give him access to young boys and their homes. My husband and I discovered a person we knew nothing about hiding behind the person we had been allowed to see. John believed the youth minister would not survive being exposed so he spent his teenage years feeling he was responsible for the youth minister's wellbeing, and that of the church. John knew it would cause much trouble if the truth was known, so he decided he should say nothing. He mentally split the youth minister into two people, an older person he liked as a friend and a foe who had taken away his rights and for whom he felt responsible.

The youth minister became engaged to a missionary who was overseas. When she returned for their wedding, he told her of his behavior towards John and she broke their engagement. She did not tell my husband or myself why she had broken the engagement or warn us, but she told the senior minister of the church. At the time John was fifteen years old. The senior minister said nothing to us either, and left John in a dangerous situation. He just shook our hands at the door each Sunday. His lack of action gave the youth minister access to my son and our home for four more years. He left the church without ever speaking to my husband or myself about the abuse, though he did speak with others.

My mother taught me that the minister was God's representative here, a spiritual leader and teacher, a person of integrity led by the Holy Spirit. I told my children this and added that the church was a place of safety, somewhere they could go for help. In my anger I asked God where He had been and why He had not acted to stop the abuse. I came to realize that God works through people and He had tried to intervene by making people aware of the situation. It wasn't God's fault John didn't have the protection he deserved. I don't have unrealistic expectations of ministers, they are human. They do, however, have a duty of care to uphold and I do expect a minister to act in an appropriate way when Christian moral principles have been violated and criminal offences have taken place. I am still disillusioned and find it difficult to have any confidence or trust in the clergy.

Two years later, John and I first received an expression of regret and assurance of love and concern from the deacons—it came by mail. Few visited, rang or gave support and encouragement in those years which were so difficult for my family. There were times when John wished he had told no-one, his fears that speaking out would cause trouble had come true, but the casualties were him and his family. We felt so isolated and alone, that we were being blamed for what had happened. There were times I felt I wouldn't survive the stress and that I couldn't provide all the help and support my sons needed. John was my first concern, his health, emotional needs, his safety, concerns for his future life; would he catch up in his development and be alright? My other sons were hurt, angry and confused. They couldn't make any sense out of what had happened. The youth minister had been someone they had looked up to, someone important in their lives, someone they had trusted. They couldn't understand him. They too have needed support and help as they have tried to sort out their own feelings about this time in their lives. It has had a deep effect on us all.

The leaders acted in the "best interests of the church." They kept things quiet and protective. The story they allowed to be told was not the truth and by doing this divisions and troubles were caused over a period of years as people responded to rumor and misinformation. There were people who wanted to help my family. When they asked for the matter to be dealt with in a scriptural way, the truth told and appropriate disciplinary action taken, they were branded as troublemakers, not fitting in, not trusting the leaders. Some left the church which had been their spiritual home. They also became casualties and for them there has been no healing. Some left because of the anger and betrayal they felt over what had happened, one because of the anxiety she felt for her child's safety in the church.

The church held a service to heal its hurt from these events. We were not invited to share in the service or be ministered to for the healing of our pain. A special meeting was called where a letter was read. There was unanimous support for a motion to "fully accept the statement by the Rev ... of these events." In the letter John was given the blame for his parents not being told, though he was only fifteen years old and still legally a minor. The writer asked people to understand that his "intentions were honorable and without selfishness" and that he wanted to "find a way through that would best help the hurt parties." Nothing he did helped John, but it did help others.

The statement read was not written by the youth minister, John or me, nor were we able to be present or to challenge the veracity of the statement. The church also resolved that "any future pastoral leadership serving in our church not be made to re-address this matter," i.e. don't talk about this any more. Again the feeling for John, who was the victim, and for his family, was that we had been dealt with without being involved. We were told of a decision made about us, but it had nothing to do with us—we were not consulted.

When a group was sent to visit us, two men and a couple arrived. The two men I only knew by sight, the couple had a son the same age as John and I thought to myself that it could have been their son instead of mine who had been sexually assaulted by the youth minister. How would they have felt, would they have coped any better than I did, would the church have cared for them? When I wanted to talk about what had happened to John, I was told the past was not to be talked about, they had come for

Bible reading and a prayer. This was the first time there had been any outreach to us in this way and it was what I had desperately needed: Christians to pray with me, to care and help me hang onto my battered faith. But I also needed to be able to talk about the past and say how I felt about what had happened to John. I knew they didn't know what had happened and for me this had to be the starting point. One of them started to talk quite sincerely about the wages of sin and I thought I would be sick. I knew the wages of sin, death and destruction—it wasn't my sin, but that of others, that had caused the destruction in the life of my family.

I believe this period in the life of the church was an opportunity for people to grow in compassion, understanding and faith. They should have felt disillusioned, angered, grieved and hurt by the actions of previous leaders. It could have been a time of confession, repentance, healing and restitution, but for this to happen people had to be open, honest and prepared to grow through the pain and sorrow. The church could say the matter has been dealt with and resolved, but for my family there has been no healing or reconciliation, the wounds have not healed. For us, it felt as if the church was saying it had to survive and get on with its life and to achieve this, it had to disassociate itself from us and not offer support.

My battered faith had been hanging by a thread but after this my spirit died and I still feel its death. I did try to go to another church but I always vomited or became upset and shaky and I didn't have enough energy to spare. Now no-one in my family has a spiritual home and in spite of us being needy people there is no one to minister to our spiritual needs.

When a young person is sexually abused by a Christian leader the personal and spiritual growth of the child is hindered. They need Christian adults who accept the responsibility of prayer, support and encouragement for them. Suicide can be a real threat. The church system seems to blame the victim for what has happened to them and it offers the perpetrator support and help because of what he has "suffered." Sin and repentance seems to be a forgotten message, while we are taught you must forgive those who wrong you. I thought the Bible spoke of repentance as a requirement before forgiveness was given. The road from sin to forgiving can be long, and filled with much anger and pain—both emotions part of the healing process.

After dealing with the immediate grief of my husband's death, I began to think about the church system. I desperately wanted to make sure other young people and families were safe. I wrote to the state church Union with a series of questions about the authority and autonomy of ministers within the church, their professional ethics and disciplinary procedures. I asked about policies and procedures when dealing with cases of sexual assault and the role of the Union within the local church.

I learnt there were no policies and procedures at all; the mechanisms to discipline a minister were loose and subjective, it was colleague investigating colleague, and the Union had no power to intervene in any church crisis unless it was invited. Some of my questions were not answered at all and I got the feeling I was being a nuisance.

The Union handled the matter quietly. What I wanted was an acknowledgment of what had happened to John and for others to be told. Most ministers were unaware of what had happened and still are. This has made me feel the church wanted to minimize what had happened. For some, without realizing it, they protected perpetrators and did not want to openly discipline colleagues.

After four years of correspondence I know the Union has had two meetings to discuss some of the issues and to begin to formulate ideas for policies and procedures and help for victims. I am sure there is opposition to many of the issues being discussed. Some ministers do not want to know that their colleagues are guilty of sexual assault, that the church is not always a safe place, or that it is indeed the concern of church leaders and not just a private matter.

Sexual assault by ministers and leaders has continued because the church has been ignorant, silent and reluctant to address the issue. I believe today the church has no option but to face the issue of sexual assault, as victims and their families will no longer be silent, they will risk everything by telling what has been done to them.

The victim's real need is for an acknowledgment of what has happened. It takes courage to tell, especially when the offender is a leader in the church. There is a desperate need for love and care from the church. Without it the victims become isolated and feel so alone they can break down: everything they believed in has been challenged and they are confused by the response of Christians to them. The church needs to care for victims as Christ did.

The Union should provide counseling for the victims, and clear rules to be followed. It should provide a person to take the role of advocate for the victim and a conciliator to work within the church to present the truth and help with the healing process.

In the long run, it won't matter how many committee meetings are held, or how fine the policies and procedures are; the victims' real need is for an acknowledgment of what has happened, to see results of actions taken by the Union, and for the local church to give them support and care.

When Christian leaders break the trust which has been given because of their position in the church, they do a great deal of damage to their victims. Positions of power and authority have been used in a way that is against the Christian calling. They have violated the rights of someone who had less power and authority.

It can take a long time and a great deal of inner strength for the victims to regain some normality in their lives and go on to become the persons God meant them to be. It is my hope that this will happen for my son John.

# CHAPTER TWELVE

# SECRET SEX—PUBLIC POWER

*T*his is a classical story of a serial abuser, whose victims possibly numbered more than one hundred. What is as disturbing as the extent of the abuse is the failure of the relevant authorities to take it seriously and to act appropriately.

*Only minor details have been altered in this account in order to preserve anonymity.*

## THE BEGINNING

When I started to try and unravel the tangled events that form this story I had no idea of what was ahead. I had no inkling that a church could harbor sexual abuse on a massive scale or go to extremes to cover it up. As some aspects of the story emerged I was shocked. At other times I felt anesthetized. I can grasp it intellectually now but it is still not easy to accept at an emotional level.

## A LONG SILENCE

Anne and I weren't going out together but our friendship was close enough so that we could sit in silence without feeling uncomfortable. After one long silence she began tentatively, "There is something that ... maybe I should tell you ... about Ron ..." With a sickening lurch I sensed that Anne had been having an affair with the minister, a married man. I don't know why I made that assumption but I was pretty sure it was on the right track. For many years I have regretted my reply: "Are you sure you want to tell me about this?" I was fairly high minded and very conscious of the dangers of gossip, so I gave Anne a chance to make sure she really wanted to tell me. She looked away and the silence lengthened. Anne didn't make a second attempt to tell me about Ron.

The memory of that conversation has haunted me in recent years and I have begun to see it in a different light. Initially it seemed that they were equals having an affair, with equal responsibility for their choices but I heard that some years later he was sexually involved with a young woman in another church. I began to wonder how much choice Anne had really had. At nineteen she was a lot younger than Ron, and his charm, talents and position gave him a great deal of power.

## STUMBLING ON A PATTERN

Recently I asked an old friend who had also attended St Mary's in the seventies if he thought that anything had ever gone on between Ron and Anne. He gave me an odd look, "I thought it was Amanda." I felt sick. Amanda was Anne's cousin and several years younger.

After a couple of weeks I rang another old friend. Without giving names I told him what I suspected. His response was chilling. He had been told that Ron had been sexually involved with two girls but knew nothing of Anne and Amanda. One of the girls was about fifteen and the other about eighteen.

With dread in my heart I picked up the phone again. It was a relief to talk to someone who had only high regard for Ron, but the next friend I rang, Sally, confirmed my fears. A friend of hers had disclosed at the time that Ron had threatened violence if she didn't keep their "affair" secret. She had watched him closely after these incidents and was suspicious when she observed him pay unusual attention to another woman. Both women were in their twenties.

Each of my friends was suspicious of Ron but was shocked when they saw the big picture. For over a decade all of them had kept quiet either out of a desire to respect confidentiality or simply to avoid gossip. Over the next few months it became evident that

Ron had had sexual intercourse or other sexual contact with at least seven girls and women from St Mary's.

## AFFAIR OR ABUSE?

Sally had thought a lot about what had happened and had decided that her friend was not really an equal partner in an "affair" but had been betrayed by a man who had played upon her lack of confidence and exploited her. He had abused his position of trust and power. To Sally this was a form of sexual abuse. She said that her friend was a survivor.

Sally warned me to think carefully before contacting other women from St Mary's, as they too might have been abused by Ron. She pointed out that it is common for women to repress such memories, that they may not have told their partners and that it was better for them to deal with these experiences in their own time.

## AN ABRUPT DEPARTURE

The people of St Mary's were very surprised when Ron left suddenly less than two years after he had arrived. A farewell was hastily arranged but only a handful knew why he was leaving. I discovered that one of the survivors had told her family about Ron and that they had quietly forced him to leave. A bit more checking revealed that he had left two previous churches "under a cloud." Hearing second-hand stories made me uneasy but I realized that it was extremely unlikely that all these accounts were false. Perhaps a bit more straight talk and openness might have curbed Ron.

## ALARM BELLS

One friend did choose to vent his concerns at the time. John led a fellowship group. He was pleased that Ron was quick to introduce himself to the fellowship members and that he offered to drive some of them home. The following week he turned up as the night concluded and drove a carload of girls home. This set alarm bells ringing for John. He informed an elder and rather nervously insisted that it stop. The elder said that he would talk to Ron. To

John's surprise Ron didn't raise the matter with him. He didn't drive girls home from the fellowship any more either.

John went on to explain the circumstances of Ron's appointment to St Mary's as he had been a member of the selection panel which had invited Ron to be our minister. They were advised by denominational headquarters that any rumors they might have heard about Ron were unfounded and were to be discounted. Actually the panel had not heard any rumors, but they accepted the advice and he was chosen.

## HIGH LEVEL COVER-UP?

When a minister told me that many people within the denomination were aware that Ron had been sexually abusive in his first appointment, back in the sixties, I wondered why so little was done to protect the girls at St Mary's. Did discretion and fear of scandal degenerate into a cover-up? It is clear that the climate of secrecy didn't help.

After leaving our church Ron went on to another appointment as a minister. Some years later his "affair" with a young woman from that church was reported to denominational leaders. Ron was confronted and his offer to resign from the position was accepted. The reasons for his resignation were not made public. Although he was not given a new post, he retained his authority to minister. He left the city.

## A DIFFICULT DILEMMA

I knew little of Ron's subsequent career but I discovered that in recent years he had been employed to teach religious studies to teenage boys and girls. He took them on camps and to his home.

For a long time I agonized over this information. It seemed wrong to sit back and do nothing. I asked several sexual abuse counselors from different agencies for advice. They were extremely concerned about the young girls Ron worked with. They felt that because I had stumbled across so many survivors with just a few phone calls it was probable that Ron had abused many others from our church and hundreds of girls and women over the decades. One counselor revealed that she already knew of his abuse through a counseling connection.

I wondered how many women had left the church because of Ron. Maybe they blamed God. Perhaps some were still carrying a "secret sin" with them, an illusion that they were the only one, that it was all their fault. Would they feel differently if they knew that Ron had manipulated many others?

Could Ron still be abusing girls and women? I felt compelled to act but I didn't know what to do. Lawyers emphasized that unless one of the survivors laid charges nothing could be done. Counselors stressed that the survivors should not be approached and should be free to act in their own time. Some churchgoers argued that Ron's interests must be safeguarded too and that gossip could be destructive. A friend wanted to confront Ron, one to one. The lawyers and counselors both said that Ron would almost certainly have been confronted privately on many occasions.

## "WHY CAN'T MEN DO SOMETHING?"

A social worker told me that sexual abuse is widespread among churchgoing families. She spoke with a weary anger, saying "It is always women who clean up afterwards." She pointed out that it is women who comfort the survivors, who spend years listening to the hurt and trying to heal the wounds. "Why can't men do something about this? It is men who are the abusers."

I didn't know what to do. Talking about it, crying, raging and praying weren't enough.

## ACTION

I wrote an account of what had happened and submitted it to a Christian magazine. The editor wouldn't publish it but the experience of writing made me see that I would have to act. I decided to approach the churches which jointly employed Ron. This was difficult as I was determined to protect the privacy of survivors. I presented what I knew of Ron's history, along with the names of clergy and counselors who could confirm details, and I emphasized the possibility that the teenage girls he worked with could be at risk.

The churches were cautious and reluctant to deal with the matter directly. It took several approaches before anyone confronted Ron. His story, that he had made "one mistake fifteen years ago," was adapted to "two affairs twenty years ago," but he was believed. This was particularly disturbing because one minister indicated that there was a recent allegation that Ron had sexually abused a girl. I wasn't reassured by the minister's assessment that the allegation appeared to be without substance. Eventually Ron's resignation was accepted "with regret" because "rumors were spreading." Many church people accepted Ron's account and felt that he had been falsely accused. They were angry that his good work was being sabotaged.

## RON CONFRONTED

I was relieved that he had been removed from his position but still felt uneasy. Arthur, who had also once attended St Mary's, was concerned that Ron would move on to a new place, perhaps switch denominations and continue the pattern. He made some inquiries and gathered further evidence of Ron's abuse. He also discovered that Ron had indeed changed denominations although he retained his standing as an ordained minister in his former denomination. Ron regularly preached at his new church.

Arthur confronted Ron privately and asked him to sign an admission of sexual misconduct with parishioners. Arthur reasoned that with a signed admission it would be harder for Ron to work his way into another position of spiritual authority and that it might curb his abuse.

Ron signed. Why? I don't know. The fact that Arthur was obviously very determined and had "done his homework" may have been important.

## RON'S NEEDS

What of Ron? The survivors' welfare must be primary, but Ron has suffered too. Originally I felt very angry with him but now have some sympathy. Counselors have pointed out that frequently abusers have themselves been abused when young. I have no idea whether or not Ron was abused, but it is clear that he has profound problems.

When Ron's superiors first learned of his abuse he had an opportunity to examine his life and change but he needed extensive assistance. I suspect that the "chastising" he received from his superiors as they gave him new appointments must have left him confused and ill-equipped to break the cycle. If Ron had been instructed to make appropriate restitution and the issues had been met squarely, he might have been able to use the crisis to turn his life around and even perhaps achieve a measure of reconciliation. Ron's superiors hadn't done him any favors by covering up for him.

A few weeks after I approached Ron's employers he came to see me and asked me to let the matter lie. He admitted that he had behaved with sexual impropriety in four different ministerial positions but said that he had received counseling and had been "healed." Promising that he would never harm anyone, he argued that he should be allowed to continue his ministry with teenage girls.

I wanted to accept Ron's assurance that he had changed, but it wasn't easy. He had made the same promises so many times in the past. His manner was sincere but he kept shifting his ground. Several times during the conversation he took responsibility for his behavior but he also claimed more than once that the girls had seduced him, that they had "made a mug" out of him.

My stomach turned as he minimized the extent of his abuse and made self-serving admissions. It became clear that he had lied to his employers just a few weeks earlier about the extent of his abuse and also to Arthur on the day he signed the admission. His technique was transparent. He would deny as much as possible and then make admissions only when the evidence was firm, each time claiming that he was making a full confession.

Ron gave no indication that he had offered to meet survivors' counseling costs or make any other form of restitution. Neither did he express concern for them. He focused on himself, on his painful feelings of guilt, his recovery and his continuing ministry for God. Sadly, I found that I just couldn't believe that Ron had fully come to terms with his abuse. I hope that he does.

## REVEREND TURNER'S REVELATIONS

Soon after Ron's visit a minister suggested that I speak to Reverend Turner who worked in a district where Ron had been employed about twenty years earlier. I was sick of the whole subject but reluctantly made the phone call.

Reverend Turner's conservative and measured manner lent weight to what he had to say. He revealed that several women had told him that Ron had sexually abused them. They had attended one of the churches which Ron had left "under a cloud." Reverend Turner said that he had "anecdotal evidence" that Ron had sexually abused "over twenty others." This claim was staggering but I remembered the predictions of the sexual assault counselors who had estimated that he may have abused hundreds of girls and women over the decades.

Whatever the true numbers, it was clear that there must be many more cases of abuse than those which had come to light through our superficial probe. With Reverend Turner's information it was possible to sketch an overview of Ron's career as a minister. It spanned the sixties and seventies and included four pastoral appointments. Each time there were complaints of sexual abuse. At St Mary's there were at least seven cases and, according to Reverend Turner, perhaps thirty from his district.

## A BETRAYAL OF TRUST

How could Ron have abused so many girls and women? It became apparent that he had contact with a large number in church fellowships and through spiritual counseling. He was ready to take advantage of the least opportunity and used his position to engineer further contact. Sometimes his approaches were rebuffed at the outset, sometimes the abuse stopped at kissing. Frequently it involved sexual intercourse.

He made a pastoral visit to one youth fellowship member when she was alone at home and complimented her on her physical appearance. He "offered support" to one particularly vulnerable woman whose husband had just left her for a homosexual relationship. Another fellowship member was reassured by him: "The more you sin, the more you can be forgiven." A number of the girls whom Ron abused were fifteen or sixteen years old. His warm engaging personality and his elevated spiritual role must have been a compelling combination for some of these young girls.

## Church Leadership Approached

Arthur and I sent a copy of Ron's admission to Reverend Morris, one of the leaders of the denomination which had originally ordained him and appointed him to ministry. We added a detailed account of his abuse and suggested that his ordination be revoked.

It seemed clear that the denominational leaders had made a mistake years earlier when they had allowed Ron to quietly resign and leave the city. If his ordination had been publicly revoked at that time he would have found it far more difficult to obtain a new position as a spiritual guide to young girls. We pointed out that because Ron was still ordained he was still in a position to go to a distant city, seek another appointment as a minister and perhaps continue to abuse.

Reverend Morris gave us a friendly reception but said that nothing could be done. Church law wouldn't allow action so many years later. He rejected every suggestion that we made. He wasn't even willing to issue a general warning about Ron to his colleagues in other cities, despite the fact that Ron had already applied to at least two regional leaders for a pastoral appointment.

It was difficult to accept that Reverend Morris wouldn't act. He had considerable personal knowledge of Ron's abuse, a signed admission and corroboration. I couldn't understand how a church leader, a man with a reputation for integrity and strict moral values, could have so little regard for the girls and women whom Ron had abused and for those whom he might abuse in the future.

Arthur and I decided to increase the pressure. Several other leaders from the denomination were approached. Their responses varied from sympathetic concern, to denial of any knowledge and responsibility, to outright hostility. "Nothing can be done after all this time and he's moved away," was a constant refrain. It sounded hollow when we discovered that Ron had not only retained his status as an ordained minister but was actually still licensed to pastor in our city. It became clear that moral and rational arguments were not enough.

## RON MAINTAINS GOOD STANDING WITH THE CHURCH

At this point a friend showed me an official church publication which included a recent photograph of church leaders at a formal church function. Ron was included. I couldn't believe it. The photograph had been used in another church periodical a few months earlier. At that time Arthur and I had written to the denomination with copies of the admission and pointed out that survivors who saw the photograph could only assume that Ron was still in good standing with the church. We had argued that favorable publicity for Ron was destructive for survivors trying to come to terms with their experience.

It was extraordinary that those who knew of Ron's abuse could meet with him at a church function in the first place. That they agreed to be photographed with him and allowed the continued publication of the photograph showed callous contempt for survivors.

## INCREASING THE PRESSURE

We approached a widening circle of church leaders, spelling out some of the details of the abuse and the cover-up. We emphasized that:

* Complaints about Ron's sexual abuse had been made to senior clergy when he was in at least four different positions back in the sixties and seventies.
* The complaints were kept secret and he was moved three times to a new church before he resigned and left the city.
* St Mary's had selected him on the basis of misleading information from the church authorities.
* Virtually nothing had been done for survivors.
* Church publications were giving Ron positive publicity despite the signed admission.

The senior clergy said they remembered very little about Ron's abuse and the complaints which had been made. In an interesting display of secular bureaucratic politics, a couple of them whose recollections were slightly stronger placed the responsibility squarely with their colleagues.

Arthur reflected later that these men had the resources, contacts and authority to conduct a thorough investigation but claimed that they "knew" very little. In contrast we had few resources or contacts and no authority but were able to piece together a clear picture. He concluded that they just didn't want to know.

At least one leader was dishonest. He told other church leaders that he was aware of "only two cases" although earlier he had admitted privately that he knew of three. Later I learned that he had personally received complaints about at least four cases and that he was aware of others.

We realized that these leaders lacked ethical imagination. They appeared to view the moral problem in terms of a flaw in Ron's sexuality. There was no indication that they grasped the gravity of his abuse of trust, power and position. Nor did any of them seem to comprehend that when the leadership failed to respond to survivors' complaints back in the sixties and seventies they compounded the original betrayal.

## LEGAL IMPLICATIONS

It was obvious that additional leverage was necessary. We started to point out the legal implications of the church's handling of the matter. Survivors might one day sue Ron. They might sue the church for repeatedly appointing him to pastoral positions when his abuse was known. They might seek damages because the church had continued to cast him in a positive light, through official invitations and publicity, thereby adding to their pain.

## RON GIVES UP HIS STANDING AS A MINISTER

The church leaders decided to act. Perhaps they feared that we would go to the mass media or take legal action. Maybe they were conscience-stricken. Ron was asked to voluntarily return his authority to minister and he agreed. This meant that he was no longer an ordained minister. Finally the women who had been abused could feel confident that the church totally rejected his abuse.

Or could they? I wasn't sure, because the church had not actually revoked Ron's ordination. He had been requested to "voluntarily" return his authority to minister. Would survivors feel that the issue was being covered up yet again? The information still wasn't public. Few of the survivors would even hear about the church's action. I raised this with a church leader who said that there were no plans to make the matter public.

## A PUBLIC ACKNOWLEDGMENT

I wrote another long letter arguing that the action be publicized and a couple of months later a brief announcement appeared in a church publication. It made no mention of sexual abuse but indicated that Ron had been asked to return his authority to minister.

It was a relief to know that the church had taken a significant step to protect those who might be at risk in the future and to distance itself from Ron's abuse. I hoped that this decision would be positive for the survivors.

The family members, friends and counselors[1] who had encouraged me to pursue the matter felt that something important had been achieved. We reviewed what had been accomplished:
* Ron had been forced to resign from a job where young girls were at risk.
* The broad pattern of his abuse had been identified and documented.
* He had signed an admission.
* His denomination had been persuaded to request the return of his authority to minister and this had been made public.

We realized that this was solid progress, especially considering that it was achieved without contacting survivors. Arthur and I had agreed that it would be invasive to approach survivors and neither of us did so.

We were pleased but I couldn't help wishing that Ron's authority to minister had been revoked at a formal hearing. This

---

[1] Project Anna was a national resource and advocacy center which pioneered a unique service. One role is to assist those who have been sexually assaulted by church officials. The advice I received from Project Anna was just, compassionate and realistic. It stood in stark contrast to the response of church leaders.

would have had a preventive effect and would have sent survivors a clearer and more powerful message of support. It was also disappointing that the church had refused to act until a great deal of pressure had been exerted.

## WHY DID THE CHURCH COVER UP THE ABUSE?

It had been a long struggle. Why was it so difficult to get devout people to take responsible action? Three reasons quickly became clear. First, many found it hard to accept the truth, that a man who appeared to be a charming, gifted and sincere minister could really have behaved so badly. Second, the leaders were intensely concerned that the image of the church and their own reputations might be tarnished by adverse publicity. They employed damage control mechanisms similar to those used by any bureaucracy. Third, they were concerned that Ron might argue that he was being maligned and take legal action against them.

## A LACK OF COMPASSION

However these factors noted above did not explain the leadership's lack of compassion. In many hours of discussion the senior clergy showed almost no concern for the survivors, apart from a few brief comments. Most of them made no reference at all to the survivors' suffering or needs. They showed no awareness that the survivors might have had to deal with deep psychological and spiritual scarring. Apparently it didn't occur to them that some of the survivors may have contracted sexually transmitted diseases from Ron, that some might have become pregnant, have raised Ron's children, had abortions or grappled with suicide.

I had hoped that the church would show survivors that it totally rejected Ron's abuse and that his attitudes were completely at odds with the rest of the Christian community. With each conversation and letter those hopes shrank.

Some of the senior clergy had hearts of stone. A couple used the phrase, "These women fantasize." This myth has frequently been advanced to discredit women and has often been effective, but it is hard to understand how it could be employed in a situation where the abuser had signed an admission.

173

I asked a number of these leaders to explain the church's decision to keep re-appointing Ron when his abuse was known. It wasn't surprising that no answers were offered but I was shocked when one said, "Even with the benefit of hindsight I don't know that I would have acted any differently." This struck me as an outrageous assessment. This man had received a complaint twenty years earlier from a relative of a young woman who had been abused by Ron. When told that others had also been abused, including a girl of "about fifteen," he declined to accept details or names. Presumably they were not offered counseling or any other assistance. Ron continued as a minister.

It is hard to avoid the conclusion that these spiritual leaders had a very low view of women and didn't really care if women were treated with contempt. It seems that the church shares some of the worst prejudices of the secular world.

In the attempt to get the church to take a responsible stand, I spoke to a lot of people about this issue and some of them indicated that other ministers from Ron's denomination were sexual abusers. I also joined an advocacy group which offers assistance to survivors of sexual abuse by church officials. Several of the members are survivors of such abuse. The advocacy group also advises churches regarding policies and protocols in this area. We began to receive complaints that other ministers from the same denomination had sexually harassed or abused women. These came from survivors, sympathetic clergy, churchgoers and from some people who had left the church. The church's official line was that sexual abuse by clergymen was extremely rare. I began to accept, however, that it was actually a widespread problem and that the cover-up of Ron's abuse was not unique.

## CHURCH LEADERSHIP IMPLICATED

I was completely unprepared in spite of all this when I was told that one of the church leaders we had dealt with in regard to Ron was himself a sexual abuser.

At first it was hard to come to terms with this even though I believed the person who told me. However, when I reviewed this official's inability to take responsible action, things began to fall into place. He had a personal agenda. Perhaps he was repressing the knowledge of his own abusive behavior or perhaps he simply couldn't afford to take a public stand because he feared exposure.

Later I learned that two more of the leaders who had failed to deal with Ron's abuse had sexually harassed women. In one case a woman who had sought help during a family crisis was assaulted. She was physically forced to endure groping and kissing.

This meant that some of the senior clergy who had handled Ron's case over the years had their own reasons for not taking a public stand. This would have been almost impossible for me to believe a few years ago; I believe it now because I trust the people who told me and because the extent of the problem has become evident. No wonder these men behaved in such a bizarre way when confronted with the matter of Ron's abuse.

## HOPE FOR THE FUTURE

Is there hope for reform within the denomination? If the church is to change it will need to listen to survivors and to learn from them. It will need to find the courage to be honest with its members about past failings. It will need to develop policies and protocols, educate clergy, train theological students and act on complaints.

Some ministers have been very concerned about the problem but have been reluctant to speak out. They face the probability of harsh repercussions if they pursue the matter publicly. Unfortunately secrecy is at the heart of the issue and authentic reform is impossible unless the problem is dealt with openly.

Where is God in all this? I'm not sure any more but the best clue for me lies in the courage and hope shown by the survivors in the advocacy group. Over the last few months they have offered support to other survivors and bravely spoken the truth despite strong opposition from some church leaders. They are living out the Gospel story in a powerful and inspirational way.

Jesus turned to the poor, the sick and the powerless and through them brought hope to the world. Today God is offering the churches a painful journey of renewal, one that can begin when the prophetic voices of survivors are heard.

# EPILOGUE

(with apologies to Jesus of Nazareth, Luke 10:25–37)

There was a church lawyer who, to disconcert Jesus, asked, "Master, what must I do to inherit eternal life?" Jesus replied, "What does the Law say?" The lawyer said, "You must love the Lord your God with your whole heart, and your neighbor as yourself." "Well done," said Jesus, "Do this and you will live."

But the church lawyer was anxious to justify himself and said to Jesus, "But who is my neighbor?" And Jesus told the following story:

> There was a woman, who had been sexually abused by her minister, and she sat in the church, her heart bleeding with betrayal, her body aching with shame, her soul tormented by feelings of guilt. And along came a senior church official who thought to himself, "I must protect the church from scandal; I must protect the reputation of the minister; she might want compensation." So he walked by without saying anything. Then along came a group of ministers and each thought to himself, "I have a liturgy conference to attend," "This is not a social justice issue" and "I have to go and give a retreat"; so they walked by without saying anything. Then a group of her fellow parishioners came by and they thought to themselves, "She really threw herself at him; she was an adult after all; the poor man was feeling lonely," and they walked by without saying anything.
>
> In despair the woman left the church and phoned a sexual assault service and was answered by a feminist counselor. And the feminist heard the pain in her voice and listened to her story of betrayal. She spoke to her soothing words which alleviated her shame and feelings of guilt. She referred her to a mutual support group for survivors of sexual abuse and she was so moved by the woman's plight that she gave the woman her home phone number, "If ever you need help, just give me a call."

Now which of these do you think acted as a neighbor to the woman?

"The one who helped her," answered the church lawyer. And Jesus replied, "Go and do the same."

# SELECT
## BIBLIOGRAPHY

Ellen Bass & Laura Davis, *The Courage to Heal: A Guide for Women Survivors of Child Sexual Abuse*, (NY; Harper Perennial, 1988).

Pamela Cooper-White, "Soul Stealing: Power Relations in Pastoral Sexual Abuse", *The Christian Century*, 20 Feb, 1991.

Laura Davis, *Allies in Healing: When the Person You Love Was Sexually Abused as a Child*, (NY; Harper Perennial, 1991).

Robert Doran, *Theology and the Dialectics of History*, (Toronto; University of Toronto Press, 1990).

Marie Fortune, *Is Nothing Sacred?: The Story of a Pastor, the Women He Sexually Abused, and the Congregation He Nearly Destroyed*, (San Francisco; Harper San Francisco, 1989).

Peter Horsfield, "Is the Dam of Sexual Assault Breaking in the Church?", *Australian Ministry*, May, 1992.

Karen Lebacqz and Ronald G. Barton, *Sex in the Parish* (Louisville; Westminister/John Knox Press, 1991).

Mike Lew, *Victims No Longer: Men Recovering from Incest and Other Sexual Child Abuse*, (NY; Perennial Library, Harper and Row, 1990).

Alasdair MacIntyre, *After Virtue* (Notre Dame; University of Notre Dame Press, 2nd ed, 1984).

Dorothy McRae-McMahon, *Being Clergy, Staying Human*, (Washington; An Alban Institute Publication, 1992).

Alice Miller, *The Drama of the Gifted Child*, (Basic Books, 1990).

*Breaking Down the Wall of Silence*, (London; Virgo Press, 1992).

*Banished Knowledge: Facing Childhood Injuries* (NY; Anchor Books, 1990).

Neil Ormerod, *Grace and Disgrace*, (Sydney; E.J. Dwyer, 1992).

Janet Pais, *Suffer the Children: A Theology of Liberation by a Victim of Child Abuse*, (Mahwah; Paulist Press, 1991).

Michael Scott Peck, *People of the Lie*, (London; Rider, 1988).

M. Pellauer, B. Chester and J. Boyajian (eds), *Sexual Assault and Abuse: A Handbook for Clergy and Religious Professionals*, (Harper, San Francisco, 1991).

James Newton Poling, *The Abuse of Power*, (Nashville; Abingdon Press, 1991).

Stephen Rossetti (ed), *Slayer of the Soul: Child Sexual Abuse and the Catholic Church*, (Mystic; Twenty-Third Publications, 1990).

Peter Rutter, *Sex in the Forbidden Zone: When Men in Power—Therapists, Doctors, Clergy, Teachers and others—Betray Women's Trust*, (London; Mandala, 1989).